Reading *Enlisted: Navigating Your Prophetic Assignment* has given me great pleasure. Foremost, because the author, Apostle Charlie Howell III, is gifted beyond his years and endowed with a great mandate from God to teach the body of Christ. Secondly, because of the anointing released in this book, which has convinced me that no matter what level you may be in your Prophetic assignment, the foundational truths outlined by Apostle Howell will advance you to your next Prophetic level. I have read numerous books on the five-fold Ministry gifts and never have I read one that has inspired me as a Pastor, as much as this one has. The reader will be inspired to become comfortable in his/her calling to the extent that they will not compare themselves among others but be driven to reach the pinnacle of the Prophetic Office God has ordained for them. I commend the author for such a balanced work.

— Dr. Juanita M. Whitfield

Apostle Charlie had produced a masterpiece which helps prophets navigate their prophetic assignment. He gives us examples from scripture of people who literally navigated their prophetic commission, mission, and ministry. He lays out the life and ministry of these patriarchs who had modeled a pattern for us as examples. As I scrolled through the manuscript, I could feel God's breath on the texture and texts of this great piece. The grammar, style, structure, and the verbiage used is typical of the prophetic expression. This work is a must read for the entire church, not just the prophets of the Lord. It is with this that I have faith in the fruit this work will produce. The good news is that Apostle Charlie did not leave us without hope. Our hope is in Jesus. He is still building His church; therefore, He is still building His prophets and this book encapsulates the mind of God.

— Dr. Oscar Guobadia

I'm telling you I could barely put this book down! Wow, is all I can say! This book is full of earth-shattering truths. Apostle Charlie really lays the foundations for anyone who is prophetic or wanting to learn about prayer, consecration, the office of the prophet, and the function and flow! This is what the Body of Christ desperately needs. Apostle Charlie has poured so much into this, and his love for God and God's people is apparent.

— Jenny Weaver

Apostle Charlie Howell III has a powerful gift to articulate the mind of God. Most books on the prophetic are a compilation of regurgitated material. This book is fresh and brings a unique perspective to prophetic ministry. *Enlisted* will help stir up your passion for Jesus by emphasizing the importance of prayer and intimacy, two missing ingredients in modern ministry. The prophetic can be complicated and theologically deep, but Charlie finds a way to communicate it in a way that even a child can understand. This book will activate you, helping you to go deeper in your assignment.

— Nathaniel Saint-Eloi

ENLISTED

Navigating Your Prophetic Assignment

CHARLIE HOWELL, III

ISBN: 9798711181248

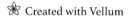 Created with Vellum

This book is dedicated to those who have been ostracized and shunned because of their prophetic gift.

TABLE OF CONTENTS

Acknowledgments	xi
Foreword	xiii
Introduction	xvii
1. Face to Face	1
2. The Call to Intercession	21
3. Ministers unto the Lord	41
4. Operation Desert Storm: How God Prepares Prophets	59
5. Operation Desert Storm: How God Equips Prophets	79
6. Operation Desert Storm: How God Sends Prophets	99
7. Same World, Different Methods	119
8. Gift, Spirit, & Office	129
Notes	141
About the Author	143

ACKNOWLEDGMENTS

I dedicate this book to Jesus, my Lord and Savior. He is responsible for my prophetic destiny and has surrounded me with individuals that have pushed me. He is my commander-in-chief and called me as a lieutenant to raise and train prophets. I honor my natural children and spiritual children who will carry this prophetic mandate until Jesus comes.

Thank you to my wife, Shanda, for being a strong woman! Not only did you give birth to our baby girl during this time of writing, but you have been a pillar as we both had the challenge of being in the NICU and managing the school, church, business, and the house. I acknowledge my mother, Edna and my mother-in-law, Faye. Both of you have been instrumental in my prophetic development—going back to the age of three and four. God used you as a catalyst to spark my prophetic interest and initiate me into prophetic dimensions and realms.

I also want to acknowledge my group of prophetic mentees and spiritual children. It is because of you that this resource was birthed. You were patient as I wrote each chapter and put a demand on the scribal anointing.

FOREWORD

I believe that the Lord is raising up a bold generation of prophetic builders. These are not those prophets who are just trying to get another word or tap into another revelation without strategic purpose. These building prophets have their ears tuned in to hear what the Lord is saying to nations and territories. I call them apostolic prophets: they are those prophets who are sent, assigned, and commissioned with a building anointing.

> "Now the boy Samuel was ministering to the LORD before Eli. And word from the LORD was rare in those days, visions were infrequent." 1 Samuel 3:1 (NASB)

Samuel was a prolific seer with abundant revelatory gifts, yet he gave his life to building. Perhaps if he had been trained in one of today's prophetic schools, he would have only become famous for his ability to see. However, this was not the plan for this great prophetic builder! God has assigned him to a place and space that was void of prophetic flow. I believe this is part of the apostolic and prophetic paradigm. We are born into moments that demand our gifts!

Samuel changed the culture of the day. He raised up a new wineskin of prophetic training and building. Let me say this in a more simplistic way: he created a new pattern! He birthed prophetic institutes. This was under the old covenant when the primary emphasis of the prophetic was to function as an oracle. The people could not hear God without the lips of the prophet. Yet Samuel understood that prophecy alone would not change the atmosphere. He recognized the need to build!

Under the New Covenant prophetic administration, prophets are speaking into the lives of people who are often able to hear God personally (if they have been born again). The dispensation has changed, and the function has changed. While prophets still live in the realm of mystery and insight, they are called by God to be masterful equippers. Every equipper needs to be equipped.

Getting equipped requires both effort and pursuit. It does not come without your involvement. This is why I believe resources like this one are so valuable. I want you to take this material and digest it so that you can be properly established in your prophetic purpose. My spiritual son, Apostle Charlie Howell III represents the new breed! He is a powerful apostolic builder with prolific prophetic function. Enjoy this writing and prepare to go to the next level.

Ryan LeStrange
Author of *Breaking Curses* and numerous other titles.
Founder of Hubs Movement, RLM, & TRIBE

INTRODUCTION

Navigating the prophetic world without structured teaching and resources can be a challenge. This book was birthed to help prophetic vessels maneuver in their calling. Growing prophetically can be difficult especially when you are a prophetic type like Samuel or David, who were caught in a transitional era. Yet, when the calling comes, it is up to the recipient to be diligent in preparation and stewardship. This is why community and leadership are so important: learning alone and in isolation is not the plan of God for new testament believers. Having comradery and guidance to evaluate teachings and structures to hold prophetic people accountable is a more excellent way for releasing mature prophetic vessels. My word to you as you move through your prophetic journey is never to give up or grow weary.

Oftentimes the word of the Lord comes to confront pre-existing thought patterns and culture. It is vital that you understand how important continual learning and development is for leaders. Your wineskin and your methodologies will be challenged as you morph into a new testament prophetic model. At the end, your speech and delivery will mimic characteristics of Jesus, our greatest prophetic example (Romans 8:29). Oftentimes the immature look at improvement and quit because they interpret it as a sign of current shortcomings or failures. But this is the wrong perspective. Instead, you should see it in terms of your growth margin, as an opportunity to update and upgrade. There is nothing like being in a techno-savvy world using primitive tools and verbiage.

If you are reading this book you are probably at some stage in your prophetic development. No one buys prophetic books and resources for fun. Prophetic people love prophetic material. Your decision to purchase this book proves that you have already enlisted in the army of the Lord, specifically into the prophetic branch. This is a serious call and a huge responsibility. Prophetic ministry is not for those who are immature, playful, or those who disregard order. In a natural army, the bulk of the responsibility falls on the mature; similarly, this prophetic calling is for the mature. The reason there are causalities and friendly fire in the prophetic is because many have put on the gear but have not spiritually suited up.

Whether you are in the beginning, middle, or end you will receive tools that will help you improve and transition from one place to the next. For veteran prophetic individuals, this book will be a refresher, giving you a jump start back into the cutting edge. You will be sharpened because iron sharpens iron (Proverbs 27:17). Set your heart and your mind to finish this book in the same season that you started. Do not jump ship but remain faithful and God will bless the fruit of your study. Get ready to hear, see, and dream. But, most importantly, get ready to meet the man that enlisted you, swore you into the prophetic branch, gave you purpose, and released you into your assignment. He longs to meet with his prophets daily, because he has a lot to say to you and through you!

1

FACE TO FACE

Growing up in the early 1990s, I was surrounded by people who had a strong prayer life. Prayer is essential to the growth of any Christian. If there is no prayer life, there is no true intimacy with God. Before we delve into the prophetic, it is vital that prophets understand that the call to prayer is the first call that must be answered. I have seen people who are ready to release the word of the Lord but have not yet stood in the counsel of God (Jeremiah 23:18). This prayer time should not be focused on intercession, which is about standing in the gap for others. Instead, it should be purely devoted to talking to your Savior about you! I need to establish this as a foundation for the rest of your prophetic journey: never confuse your devotional and personal prayer with intercession. Intercession is what we do as service to God; prayer is what should be done because one loves God. It is from the place of prayer that your heart will be transformed, the fruit of the spirit is developed and ripened, eyes are detoxed from this worldly system, and revelation and mystery unfold.

This must remain a priority in everything that you do. Oftentimes as one grows in Christ, their focus shifts from the Kingdom to what the Kingdom produces. Prayer or intimacy with God puts Christ on the throne and helps us magnify and prophesy from a seated place. Matthew 6:33 gives us clarity that we should seek the Kingdom and everything else will then be added. The Kingdom has everything to do with the King of Glory, Jesus. Jesus' death will have been in vain if there is no oneness with our beloved Savior. Consider the veil of the Old Testament. It separated us from Him. The mystery of the new is that the King died so that he can live in us and vice versa. Your objective is not to take his bloodshed for granted. His death means nothing if there is no intimacy. His death means nothing if there is a middle-man. His death means nothing if there isn't a daily seek. As a prophetic vessel, your greatest encounters with our Lord should be in the privacy of your own home. Even now as you read, your passion, zeal, and fervor are being ignited to seek the secret place and dwell there.

If you show me a prophet, I will show you a pray-er. A prayerless prophet is a dangerous and probably false one. The lack of accuracy does not make one a false prophet, a bad heart does. Prophets should be the strongest pray-ers in a church, organization, or business. Consider very quickly prophetess Anna in the Bible. According to Luke 2, Anna did not depart from the temple because she was praying night and day. This is a strong indication that prophets are not just people who speak for God. They are individuals who are not above worship, communication, and daily submission to the service of God. There are individuals who are drafted into the house of God and begin working without first building a solid relationship with Christ. There are people who were once in love with Jesus but have since lost their first love. The spirit of religion reigns in a church or a community whenever works and things are treasured more than a relationship with God. I remember growing in the prophetic and having a sense that I had "arrived." Information sometimes can do that to your head, blow it up. It is a Luciferian mindset. Well, let me tell you that God quickly pulled my tail back in! Again, it is prayer that makes one wise. I am reminded of the lamp and the oil that the 10 virgins had. Prayer keeps oil in your lamp. It allows you to see the King coming in his glory. It illuminates your path. It allows you to hear his voice and not an echo of it.

Those who carry prophetic mantles always have a strong track record of prayer. In most cases, prayer was the thing that initiated many into their callings. Becoming prophetic is not a badge of honor; being a person of prayer is the greatest honor that one can receive. Prayer is NOT begging God for something, but instead, it is simply having constant and meaningful communion with our precious Savior. This is what grants us conversation, transformation, and authority. This call is the greatest call, and it is from this place that true sons and daughters are circumcised, birthed, and thrust into destiny. Any elevation outside of prayer is a pseudo one. Consider the life of our Lord and Savior, Jesus. He passed through prayer at the Garden of Gethsemane before enduring the cross (Matthew 26:36). It was this place of prayer that gave him the strength to yield to and endure such a hard task. Elevation came, but prayer came first! Woe unto a generation of people who desire the platform but vacate knee bone valley!

Before I proceed to discuss the ways in which the prophetic and prayer are synonymous, I want to charge you with understanding that prayer is for every BELIEVER! You should not try to opt out of prayer and become "regular." This is a high calling and to be like Jesus is to be a person of prayer. Paul told us to rejoice always and to pray without ceasing (1Thessalonians 5:16). Consequently, a nice attitude is connected to prayer. Being a crocodile prophet reveals that the person needs to enter into the chambers and allow prayer to transform them. NOTE, intercession without a prayer life will make one mean and nasty! So, if you close this book or stop reading, the call to prayer will still be calling your name. Those who answer it will be thrust not only into the prophetic, but into a face-to-face encounter with God!

Abraham

Abraham's placement as God's prophet was connected to his ability to pray. Genesis 20:7 (ESV) speaks of him, saying, *"Now therefore, restore the man's wife: for he is a prophet, and he will pray for you and you shall live. But if you do not restore her, know that you shall surely die, you and all who are yours."* This text illustrates the connection between prophets and prayer, revealing that all prophets should have both a prayer dimension and a supernatural dimension. In this context, Abraham's prayer revealed that the prophet's position can be pivotal to those who are in authority and that prophets should have a clean heart to easily administer the power and authority of God. Long gone are the days where the expectation is for Apostles to be the only ones who administer healing to individuals. Moreover, our responsibility to pray supersedes any personal offenses that we have towards individuals, organizations, or those in authority.

Moses

Moses is a popular prophetic example from the Old Testament. He heard directly from God and developed a very strong relationship. His encounters with God include powerful manifestations in the earth which resulted in the children of Israel coming out of Egypt on their way to the promised land. Their very existence and survival from the Egyptian army demonstrates the way that Moses' leadership rested in his relationship with God. He asked God to show him His glory! In other words, he asked God not for a prophetic word or any worldly thing, but simply for His presence.

Moses had a sister named Miriam who was also a prophet. The relationship that God established with her was different than the one He established with Moses. While God spoke face-to-face with Moses, He did not do the same with Miriam. God spoke to Moses as a friend speaks to a friend, therefore showing us that prophets with the strongest relationships are those who constantly speak to and hear directly from God himself.

Numbers 12:1-2 (ESV)

"*Miriam and Aaron spoke against Moses because of the Cushite woman whom he had married, for he had married a Cushite woman. And they said, 'Has the Lord indeed spoken only through Moses? Has he not spoken through us also?' And the Lord heard it."*

Numbers 12:6-9 (ESV)

"And he said, 'Hear my words: If there is a prophet among you, I the Lord make myself known to him in a vision; I speak with him in a dream. Not so with my servant Moses. He is faithful in all my house. With him I speak mouth to mouth, clearly, and not in riddles, and he beholds the form of the Lord. Why then were you not afraid to speak against my servant Moses?' And the anger of the Lord was kindled against them, and he departed."

Moses had such a strong relationship with God. Like Moses, those who enter the place of prayer are given strong clarity and access to prophetic rivers. According to Numbers 12:6-9, dark sayings and riddles are not the summation of conversation with those who dare to say yes to the call of intimacy with Jesus. Another benefit of intimacy and friendship with God is that Christ is our defender. Your prophetic mantle has an angelic and heavenly guard that fights against those who fight against you. Although there are several instances in the Bible of Moses stepping into intercession, there is a wonderful example of Moses paying attention to a personal encounter with Christ. Exodus 33:18 (ESV) happens to be my favorite scripture; it is here that Moses begged God *"please show me your glory."* As much as we desire to talk to God for others, prophets and prophetic people must always remember that you need Jesus just as much as others do. So, it is important that you break the cycle of ignorance and learn to spend time with Christ so that your life will not be solely predicated on someone else having to pray to God on your behalf. Just like with Moses, God can talk to and commune with you face-to-face.

Elijah

Elijah is probably one of the most revered prophets in the Old Testament. Many prophetic people desire to be like him and often compare their prophetic personalities to his. However, if you look at it, Elijah had a plethora of issues as a prophetic vessel, but I will save that particular discussion for a later chapter. While Jesus should be the greatest example for those who are desiring a certain prophetic type, Elijah's example and pinnacle of movement in the Old Testament can be summarized by a New Testament reflection. James 5:16 (ESV) states that *"Elijah was a man with a nature like ours, and he prayed fervently that it might not rain, and for three years and six months it did not rain on the earth. Then he prayed again, and heaven gave rain, and the earth bore its fruit."* This illustrates the great authority that a believer has when willing to get down on their knees and talk to God. When someone who is close to God speaks, the earth responds because the language, authority, and power of attorney have been transferred from the Father to us as ambassadors in Christ.

James 5:16c (ESV) states that *"the prayers of a righteous person has great power as it is working."* Righteousness is not found in works; righteousness is an individual. It is the person of Jesus the Christ. When you go into prayer as a prophetic person, Christ is revealed, and you begin to adopt his nature. Thus, he is the one who is righteous through you. Oftentimes, the lack of purity, cleanliness, and the presence of perversion are stone walls that prevent people from having their prayers answered. The writer James shows us that there is no difference between Elijah and us. He was a regular human being, not superman. Even understanding the dispensation of time gives modern believers an upper hand. We have the righteous One living on the inside of us. The elements, nature, and conditions are all waiting for the word of the Lord. As a matter of fact, the earth is groaning for the manifestation of the sons of God (Romans 8:19)!

Samuel

As a prophet and judge, Samuel was birthed out through prayer. His first encounter with the presence of God was initiated through servitude and him being dedicated to the service of God. This reveals that there must be a perfect marriage between servitude and the presence of God. One without the other creates a false balance. I remember growing up and working so diligently for God. I would spend hours reading scriptures, playing the piano, and singing. These times were spent carrying out religious order, but they were void of the presence of God. Consequently, things in my life were halted and the prophetic was hindered because there was no intimacy with the Lord.

Reading the Bible requires the assistance of the Holy Spirit. He is the one that gives revelation and makes the Word known. Consider the significant amount of time that Samuel had to spend in prayer in order to be able to hear the Lord clearly enough to distinguish when He was calling him (1 Samuel 3:2-8). These times came because Samuel had a yearning for the presence of God. 1 Samuel 3:3 (ESV) speaks of the first time that God called Samuel. Here, *"The Lamp of God had not gone out, and Samuel was lying down in the temple of the Lord, where the ark of God was."* Samuel understood the importance of merely being in proximity with the ark (presence) of God. This suggests that even when things look dim, if you posture yourself near the light, not only will you be on the cutting edge, but you will also stay clear of the cut that God is getting ready to make. Samuel's prophetic journey did not end with prayer, however, that was just the beginning. As a child, his responsibility was to minister unto the Lord, not to engage in intercession. The wisdom here is that beginners can be easily crushed under intercession when they have not yet matured. In the next chapter, we will see how one's responsibility shifts from prayer into a greater measure once they are secure and stable in their walk with Christ.

Daniel

Daniel was a great prophetic prototype for everyone to pattern themselves after. He was a man of influence, affluence, prestige, and authority. There was enough jurisdiction and rank in Daniel's mantle to charge angels and disrupt an entire nation. Daniel was set apart due to prayer. His prayer life was coupled with fasting, which in the realm of the spirit can cause many things to shake and quake! One of the things I want to point out about Daniel is his infatuation with secrets. Notice that secrets are reserved for the secret place. This place is not a common place that all can enter, but those who do must understand confidentiality and abide by a stricter standard that sets them apart from the majority.

Consider Daniel 2:17-19 (ESV), which says, *"Then Daniel went to his house, and made the decision known to Hananiah, Mishael, and Azariah, his companions, that they might seek mercies from the God of heaven concerning this secret, so that Daniel and his companions might not perish with the rest of the wise men of Babylon. Then the secret was revealed to Daniel in a night vision. So, Daniel blessed the God of heaven."* Daniel was a man of prayer. His livelihood relied upon communication and special intel from God. This is not the very first time that Daniel was in a prayer hold! The cares of this world oftentimes will push people into a holding pattern, and it is the secrets of God that will release their breakthrough.

Daniel 2:17-19 reveals the importance of prayer communities. When wise, prophetic people come together for a cause, heaven responds. This is a triple assault on the demonic realm and there is nothing that eagles and prophetic watchers will not see, discern, or sense in the spirit. As a pray-er, the best place you can ever be is in the war room. That is where wars are won. Also notice that Daniel went to HIS HOUSE to pray. Prayer has an epicenter: privacy! Consider what Jesus told the religious people of his day: when you pray go to your room and shut the door (Matthew 6:6). God rewards those who come to him without trying to be seen! Remember that humility will increase your sight, your potency, and will ultimately dictate what level of secrets God will entrust you with.

Jesus

Jesus—fully God and fully man—understood the necessity of prayer! While still being divine, his human side showed and depicted why we should be people of prayer. Jesus not only prayed, but he coupled it with Spirit-led fasting. The first recorded time that Jesus prayed is often missed in the Bible because of the events surrounding it. Jesus prayed and something huge happened: the Bible says that the heavens were opened. When you pray in your identity as a son or daughter, heaven opens. The specific words that Jesus said during his prayer were not mentioned, and I do not believe they were even that important. Luke 3:21 (ESV) states, "*When all the people were baptized, it came to pass that Jesus was also baptized; and while He prayed, the heavens was opened.*" Notice here that heaven was not opened after he prayed, but *during* His prayer. For those of you who go to God and feel like nothing is reaching him, let this be an encouragement that the response you need is already on the way.

Jesus modeled the perfect marriage of prayer and assignment. When there is constant communication with the Father, completing an assignment is not hard. Prayer keeps an individual yielded to the mandate that God has called them to. Consider what would have happened if Jesus had waited to communicate to the Father only at Gethsemane (Matthew 26:2-36). It would have made the task even more challenging. Yet, he was able to yield to his assignment because this was not his first time entering into prayer, nor was it the first time that this was a battle between two wills. In the model prayer, Luke 11:2 (ESV), Jesus says when you pray you should say *"your will be done."* Prayer keeps prophetic and apostolic people in their assignments. It keeps their wills out of the way and always brings God's will to the forefront. A prayerless prophet is one who will walk in disobedience, confusion, and division. Additionally, there is often a discipline issue with individuals who do not pray. Jesus says to pray, for *"the spirit is indeed willing, but the flesh is weak"* (Matthew 26:41, ESV). Prayerlessness always reveals a FLESHLY believer.

The last nugget of wisdom that Jesus gives to us is that your prayer life is something that should be seen and witnessed by those close to you. This does not mean that you pray for recognition, but rather, when a prayer life cannot be detected there is danger in the camp. Jesus modeled prayer with such presence that the disciples wanted to know the secret. Luke 11:1 (ESV) says, *"Now Jesus was praying in a certain place, and when he finished, one of his disciples said to him Lord, teach us to pray, as John taught his disciples."* By waiting until Jesus had finished, the disciple reveals that this time of prayer was a protected time. Before you go into prophetic lanes, you must go into prayer.

It will make the ride smoother and the journey sweeter.

Barnabas, Simeon, Lucius, Manaen & Saul

Acts 13:1-3 (ESV)

"Now there were in the church at Antioch prophets and teachers, Barnabas, Simeon who was called Niger, Lucius of Cyrene, Manaen a lifelong friend of Herod the tetrarch, and Saul. While they were worshiping the Lord and fasting, the Holy Spirit said, 'Set apart for me Barnabas and Saul for the work to which I have called them.' Then after fasting and praying they laid their hands on them and sent them off."

Acts 13:4 (ESV)

"The two of them, sent on their way by the Holy Spirit, went down to Seleucia and sailed from there to Cyprus."

The prophets and teachers listed in these verses were important to the church at Antioch (the first church) because they were all prophets who were placed in local houses of worship. When prophets are raised up in houses but then vacate their call to prayer, it can lower their level of sight, timing, and precision. The company of prophets and teachers were able to release a word from the Lord concerning Barnabus and Saul, thus separating and sending them on an apostolic assignment. Imagine what would have happened if their souls were intertwined when receiving this mandate. Think briefly about how often prophetic people mix their soulish desires with prophetic words. This was not the case here. These men of God had to yield so that God could release—and ultimately shake the earth with—Saul's mandate. Thus, this scripture reveals how the prophetic and apostolic work together. Apostolic work is not exclusive from prophetic ministry. Prayer, fasting, and separation were essential in this process. When prophetic circles are birthed to only prophesy, they will miss the whole counsel of God.

The counsel and the mind of God is privy to those who dare to enter the secret place, corporately as well as individually. God sends from the ascension realm, He releases from the ascension realm, and He backs up his word from the ascension realm. Notice that the next verse, Acts 13:4, reiterated that Barnabas and Paul were not sent by prophets. The prophets may have given a word, but it was the Holy Spirit who backed up what was said in the place of prayer. Leveraging the word through prayer assures its accuracy and connects the word with heaven, ultimately pushing individuals into their divine destinies.

Paul and Silas

Acts 16:16-18 (ESV)

"As we were going to the place of prayer, we were met by a slave girl who had a spirit of divination and brought her owners much gain by fortune-telling. She followed Paul and us, crying out, 'These men are servants of the Most High God, who proclaim to you the way of salvation.' And this she kept doing for many days. Paul, having become greatly annoyed, turned and said to the spirit, 'I command you in the name of Jesus Christ to come out of her.' And it came out that very hour."

Paul and Silas, both carried out an apostolic mandate and experienced resistance while preaching the gospel. As they traveled throughout the region, they encountered a slave girl who operated under the spirit of divination, which is an anti-prophetic spirit that attacks the prophetic and apostolic. See, the grace that Paul and Silas walked in shifted the economic system of that area; therefore, the opposition that they were up against landed them in solitary confinement. However, there is always a remedy to tight places; it is the power of Jesus. There is a marvelous lesson to be learned when life hits you hard and when demonic opposition surrounds you. You can always use the word of God, of course, but the best comeback is simply to create an atmosphere for God to step into the tight place with you. Instead of speaking the word, Paul and Silas invited the Word into their space, and what once was a tight place became a place of liberation and freedom.

Paul and Silas were on the way to the place of prayer when this opposition came. Some of the things that you are up against were designed to stop you from entering into that place called prayer. Liberation came for them because they decided to rock the jail with prayer and praise. Acts 16:25-25 (ESV) tells us that at *"about midnight Paul and Silas were praying and singing hymns to God, and the prisoners were listening to them, and suddenly there was a great earthquake, so that the foundations of the prison were shaken. And immediately all the doors were opened, and everyone's bonds were unfastened."* As Paul and Silas show us, prayer is not necessarily confined to a specific room. It can and should occur anywhere and everywhere. Prayer, coupled with songs of praise, creates a BIG God. It glorifies God and not the problem. Singing for God and singing to God are two completely different modes. One is servitude, while the other is worship and adoration. One gets people up; the other gets God up! And that is exactly what happened!

Conclusion

Oh, that a church will rise in prayer! The call to prayer is for all believers, but most importantly, it is for those who desire to move in the prophetic. As a foundational piece of the prophetic, you should always be intentional about your prayer life. Even if prayer time feels "forced" in the beginning when you first start your journey, love, passion, and zeal will come along very soon. Begin each day by merely asking God to direct your steps. Never move without consulting God and you will find that prayer wheel turning in your spirit once again. Let praying prophets arise, not tomorrow but today! This begins with you. Now that you have a grasp of prayer, let us proceed to level two. Note that this next mandate—intercession—has been given primarily to the prophets.

THE CALL TO INTERCESSION

Being devoted to prayer should be the first level that individuals pass through before receiving a much weightier assignment: that of an intercessor. Prayer keeps individuals grounded in Christ, while intercession is what an individual does after having become more like Christ. See, intercession requires us to have received His desire to save, rescue, and stand in the gap for others. To be like Jesus is to be an intercessor. This position of servitude is the nature of our Lord and Savior. The entire Godhead can be seen completing this mandate throughout the Bible. While intercession is a call for everyone, the best intercessors are usually prophets. All prophets are intercessors, but not all intercessors are prophets. Understanding that statement should guide individuals toward realizing that prophets are strategically placed in areas to see, secure, and uphold the Kingdom of God.

Recognizing the call to intercession is important. Nations, regions, churches, and the world are in desperate need of voices to partner with heaven concerning what should be done next or when to stand in the gap. Ezekiel 22:33 (ESV) states, *"and I sought for a man who should build up the wall and stand in the breach before me for the land, that I should not destroy it, but I found none."* The church is full of people who are ready to pray into the microphone in public, but few are willing to cry out in compassion concerning their own communities. Having the heart of Jesus is very important when entering into intercession, which again, is a much deeper level of prayer.

I remember growing up and being done unjustly. I would ignorantly pray dangerous prayers calling on speedy vengeance and damnation against "flesh and blood." Prayers rooted in revenge do not glorify God, nor do they reflect the heart of God. Consider the mandate of intercession. It predates the origin of men. It is a decision to love humanity and pray for Christ to intervene in the affairs of men, bringing hope and reconciliation to this world. The way Jesus interceded for humanity is so beautiful. We are here in the earth as intercessory statements to the devil that the kingdoms of this world shall become the Kingdom of our Lord (Revelation 11:15). Intercession is a burden. We must take the call personally and always remember to see people the way God sees them: through love and compassion.

Intercession is a burden that must be followed through with. When you are called and stationed, you should never neglect your assignment. It would be wonderful if you could set yourself as a watchmen or intercessor. However, God called you and placed you on the wall. God set you as such so you work under his orders. Being called as an intercessor also means you get up whenever you are on duty. I remember when I was first being awakened at night around 2 and 3 AM. Instantly, I would report to social media or desire to have a conversation instead of reporting to duty, when in reality, this was supposed to be a time of intercession. God woke me up with vivid visions and dreams that were on the international, national, regional, community, and familial levels. There would be burdens surrounding natural disasters. God desires intercessors to pray these things to an end.

It is through intercession that things are obstructed, hindered, and brought to nothing. Yet, there are people who have lost their burden to intercede. This burden should not be pushed off on others as it is the birthing place for a move of the Spirit. Consider this scripture, Amos 3:7 (ESV) which says, *"For God does nothing without revealing his secret to his servants the prophets."* God reveals to his prophets what is getting ready to happen and gives them remedies through intercession. Everything you see does not have to happen; it can be overturned. God desires for you to stand in the gap so that the bad can be reversed (Ezekiel 22:30; Genesis 18:17-33).

Do not take what people do personally, but you should always take your calling and mandate from God personally. For example, if you are called to a local church, pray for the vision of that house regardless of whether or not you will be recognized, accepted, or favored. I find it very common that people will vacate their local assignments because someone else may not see their value. This is a grave mistake. If people allow offense to set in, it will hinder or frustrate the institution of the local church. If you are called to pray for a business, being stationed there as an intercessor is important. You are called by God, not by man. Jesus interceded for the very people who rejected him. Imagine if He would have decided not to go to the cross simply because the people who he was dying for had rejected him. Jesus was rejected, yet He followed through with a powerful act of intercession. Because of his obedience and humility, He was given a name that is above every name.

Anyone can come up with a good reason to avoid praying for someone. Someone may have stolen from you or hurt your feelings, but that should not cause your intercession to cease. Jesus only saw the good in people. He showed us the best example when knowing beforehand everything that we would do to him, he still died for us. We must find a way to see the good in people, even when the bad is all we can see. It is actually a sin to have an assignment in prayer and neglect it. I Samuel 12:23 (ESV) states, *"Moreover, as for me, far be it from me that I should sin against the Lord by ceasing to pray for you, and I will instruct you in the good and the right way."* Good, bad, or indifferent, the world is in the redemption plan of God. To casually allow people to slip through our fingers and hell to wreak havoc in our communities is negligent. If hell is here on earth, it is only because the church has allowed it. We have been given the keys. Jesus already preached a revival in hell; it has been conquered. As a people, we must walk in our authority by forbidding, cancelling, and voiding the works of Satan.

II Kings 13:20-21 (ESV)

"So Elisha died, and they buried him. Now bands of Moabites used to invade the land in the spring of the year. And as a man was being buried, behold, a marauding band was seen and the man was thrown into the grave of Elisha, and as soon as the man touched the bones of Elisha, he revived and stood on his feet."

THERE ARE lives at stake when prophetic people die: whether it is a natural death or when prophetic people (intercessors) refuse to walk out their God-given mandate. Notice that Elisha's mantle was a supernatural hedge that protected the region that he was stationed in. It was only when he died that Israel was invaded. You cannot afford to sleep, die prematurely, or play dead. When you do, things creep in. Although his death revived a dead man, this chapter does not speak of any successor that was left to carry on his assignment. Note, just like we raise up prophets, we should also raise up people with intercessory mantles who are called to shamar.

According to the *Blue Letter Bible*[1], the word shamar means to keep, guard, or watch. It is a word that has an intercessory flavor and aroma. The first example shown in the Bible is in Genesis 2 with Adam and Eve. God gave them the charge to shamar Eden. Their instructions were to keep, guard, and protect this preserved place. This term has every implication of prophetic hedges and intercessory walls. Their charge to watch, keep, and dress the garden was due to the diabolical assignment of Satan, the snake. Thus, when there are no intercessors who are keeping, monitoring, or watching, the local church is in trouble. Like Adam and Eve, we must learn obedience. Obedience does not mean finding loopholes, but rather, it is being cautious and careful not to eat or touch what God has forbidden. Assignments and destinies are in the balance when disobedience is caressed.

Some of the worst intercessors are the dirtiest, not because they have not received the call to intercede, but because they can never effectively war for others when they have not had their own victory over sin and the flesh. Consequently, the lack of prayer is a perpetual door for sinful intercessors. Unfortunately, they cannot pray for cities because their time is spent asking for forgiveness over dead works. Adam and Eve taught us something very powerful: that dominion and the call to intercession is not enough. People will enter into a fallen state if they are not married to obedience and if their communication lines are opened to demonic chatter. Prophets and intercessors, you must first guard your ears and eyes before they can effectively guard the place where God has stationed them!

Psalms 24:7-10, (ESV)

"Lift up your heads, O gates! And be lifted up, O ancient doors, that the King of glory may come in. Who is this King of glory? The LORD, strong and mighty, the LORD, mighty in battle! Lift up your heads, O gates! And lift them up, O ancient doors, that the King of glory may come in. Who is this King of glory? The LORD of hosts, he is the King of glory! Selah."

INTERCESSORS—THOSE who are watchers and gate-
keepers—must have a clear focus. One of the worst
things you can have on your team is a dreary intercessor. In Psalms 24 (ESV), after the prophet David
discussed how to ascend to the hill of the Lord, he
shifted his focus to how we can bring heaven down to
earth. Oftentimes, Christians have an escapism
thought pattern as it relates to intercession. Prayer for
important things is glossed over or left alone because
the 21st century church has raised up a fleet of individuals who are expecting the world to end tomorrow. As
a result, no one prays for the Kingdom to come. There
are no forward-looking prayers because various escha-
tological teachings have inadvertently trained the
saints to only expect the second coming. In reality,
however, Jesus desires to visit our church and occupy
our world daily. There is a camp of individuals who
believe Jesus' coming to be synonymous with the worst
times ever. However, I believe there are individuals
whose heads God desires to lift in order to open the
gates and doors of their cities and regions for the
biggest transformation ever. If the intercessors will lift
their heads, Christ can prepare His beautiful bride for
a glorious matrimony.

Metaphorically, the gates and doors have everything to do with the King coming inside. This is a
divine picture that should encourage all intercessors.
When the focus is always on the devil and what he is

doing, the King and his majestic train is on the outside, acknowledged but confined to the outside. Great moments are captured when intercessors have lifted heads! I remember sitting at a stop light once with my head down looking at my phone. The light changed and I did not realize it because I was distracted and my focus was on something else. Oftentimes, the enemy is a distraction to the undefeated King. If God is invited into the situation, the battle is won, situations are turned around, cancer is healed, crooked placed are made straight, angelic realms are seen and discovered, and the glory dimension is embraced.

Abraham

Genesis 18:17-21 (ESV)

"The Lord said, 'Shall I hide from Abraham what I am about to do, seeing that Abraham shall surely become a great and mighty nation, and all the nations of the earth shall be blessed in him? For I have chosen him, that he may command his children and his household after him to keep the way of the Lord by doing righteousness and justice, so that the Lord may bring to Abraham what he has promised him.; Then the Lord said, 'Because the outcry against Sodom and Gomorrah is great and their sin is very grave, I will go down to see whether they

*have done altogether according to the outcry that has
come to me. And if not, I will know.'"*

One of the first examples we see of intercession is
in the life of Abraham. In Genesis 12, Abraham left the
land of Ur and took his nephew Lot with him. Because
of expansion, Lot and Abraham separated. Lot pitched
his tent toward Sodom and Gomorrah, while Abraham
chose a different territory. Lot was a person of interest
to Abraham because he was his nephew. God's relationship with Abraham was so strong that before
destroying the city, God conversed with Abraham,
knowing that Lot was inside. Abraham asked God to
spare the city because there was a chance that there
were righteous individuals living inside. In other
words, he interceded for this nation. In the conversation, Abraham considered the good over the bad and
used it as leverage when dialoguing with God.

Here, we see the judgement of God against Sodom
and Gomorrah, but we also see a beautiful picture of
the power of intercession. Because of Abraham, Lot
and his family were escorted out of the region and
were saved. A lineage was preserved due to one man's
selfless conversation and time with God. Interestingly, I
am sure if the outcry of the city made it to heaven,
Abraham heard it as well. He had compassion for the
nation. There are realms of intercession that release
angelic assistance. Never allow a perceived outcome to

make you think that your stance in intercession is pointless. Things could have been much different as a result of your intercession.

Moses

True intercession causes things to turn. Moses dealt with multiple circumstances in which he displayed a strong intercessory grace. The first instance was when familiarity rested upon those who were following him. Aaron and Miriam offended God by asserting that they were able to hear from God too, which ultimately defied God's purpose in having a chosen man. The Lord's anger was kindled against them and Mariam became leprous and was eventually separated from the camp. Moses' response was so Messianic and revealed the heart of Jesus. He could have gloated in the fact that God punished those who disrespected his own leadership, yet he chose an unpopular route. Moses interceded for Aaron and Miriam, and the punishment lifted (Numbers 12:13-15). True intercession goes beyond personal offense. It is the walk of maturity in Christ.

The second intercession that Moses performed reveals the heart of true apostolic and prophetic people. Moses was a deliverer, a prophet, and an apostolic type. He was a builder and a writer. He went up the mountain and had a strong encounter with God. While he was away, those under his leadership decided to throw a party and revert back to the Egyptian gods. This displeased God. These are the same Israelites who had grumbled and complained every step of the way as Moses led them into the promise land. As an intercessor, Moses reminded God of his word and his promise. Exodus 32:13-14 (ESV) describes Moses as saying, *"Remember Abraham, Isaac, and Israel, your servants, to whom you swore by your own self, and said to them, I will multiply your offspring as the stars of heaven, and all this land that I have promised I will give to your offspring, and they shall inherit it forever.' And the Lord relented from the disaster that he had spoken of bringing on his people."*

One of the most powerful weapons in the hands of an intercessor is the word of God. Reminding God of his promises will cause things to progress. The word of God is the sword of the spirit (Ephesians 6:17). This is the only offensive weapon mentioned in Ephesians 6. Defensive techniques will, at the most, result in a tie, whereas the word of God is ammunition against the devil! This tool is not outdated or primitive; it is primary! This strategy is necessary for intercessors and is a great tool to place in the arsenal of all prayer warriors.

Amos

Amos 7:1-2(ESV)

"This is what the Lord God showed me: behold, he was forming locusts when the latter growth was just beginning to sprout, and behold, it was the latter growth after the king's mowings. When they had finished eating the grass of the land, I said, 'O Lord God, please forgive! How can Jacob stand? He is so small!'"

Through a vision, Amos saw that there would be no harvest as the King got his portion and the locusts were coming to eat everything left that was green. There was a plea from Amos to God for forgiveness as he knew that what was getting ready to hit the people would be too much for them to bear. He had empathy for others' situations. Oftentimes, I have observed that it can be very difficult for individuals to intercede for others when they are walking in pride and are not able to step into another's shoes. This must be conquered if we desire to see real change in the earth. Because of Amos, God relented. Intercession can literally cause people to stand, even when they are the most deserving of a great fall.

Joel

Poetically, Joel began to write about the challenges of the people (Joel 1:17-20). He wrote in order to cause the drought to end. This shows us that when we go to God with a complaint concerning the status of the land, it is intercessory in nature. People often talk to people about things, instead of petitioning God to fix them. Gossip enters into their rings and they gloat about people's issues. In his prose, Joel writes concerning the condition. His complaint and cry were extensive with example after example that eventually moved God to end the drought. It also gave strategy to the people concerning what they should do to get in right standings with the Father (Joel 2:15-16). God's response revealed the power of intercession. Joel 2: 18-19 (ESV) states, *"Then the Lord became jealous for his land and had pity on his people. The Lord answered and said to his people, 'Behold, I am sending to you grain, wine, and oil, and you will be satisfied; and I will no more make you a reproach among the nations.'"*

Anna

Luke 2:36-38, (ESV):

"And there was a prophetess, Anna, the daughter of Phanuel, of the tribe of Asher. She was advanced in

years, having lived with her husband seven years from when she was a virgin, and then as a widow until she was eighty-four. She did not depart from the temple, worshiping with fasting and prayer night and day. And coming up at that very hour she began to give thanks to God and to speak of him to all who were waiting for the redemption of Jerusalem."

Prophetess Anna is a clear example of a prophet with a prayer and intercessory mandate. She was one who served God through intercession. Her station and duty were that of a watchman set by God to pray His will into the earth. We can see Anna's entrance and exit in the biblical text once she confirmed what she had seen about Jesus in the spirit. As a people, we must be diligent like Prophetess Anna, praying continuously and staying stationed at the call of duty until our assignments are complete. Notice that her entire role prophetically was intercessory in nature. As a watchman, stay on your post and do not be moved by other prophetic types. If you are assigned to pray a specific thing through, you cannot make someone else feel your burden. This was a burden that was hers alone, thus, she pressed in and saw it to the end.

Jesus

Jesus depicted the perfect attributes of intercession. Being fully God and man, he knew how to follow through with a redemptive story. Thinking briefly about the beginning of mankind, we can see that he chose intercession from the very start. The lamb was slain before the foundations of the world, not afterwards (Revelations 13:8). Jesus made this choice, knowing we would need redemption, knowing we would mess up, knowing we would waver, yet he still decided to intercede on our behalf. If Christ can do this for us, what makes it so hard for us to pray for other hard cases? Intercession is something the believer must say yes to. Jesus proved that this call will get you a seat in the Kingdom.

Walking in the earth, Jesus had a prophetic moment. He saw that Satan desired to have Peter, but He said something that is pivotal for believers to understand: He said, "BUT, I pray for you." This prayer must be something beyond mere talking. It must be hedgy in nature. It must carry a force that can counter the attack of the devil, and it requires a lot of work. Peter and Judas made the same mistake, yet the result was different. Intercession made all of the difference. Romans 8:34 (ESV) asks us, *"Who is to condemn? Christ Jesus is the one who died—more than that, who was raised —who is at the right hand of God, who indeed is inter-*

ceding for us." Even today, years after the cross, Jesus is still interceding for us. There are times when we do not know what to pray. Jesus and His Spirit—the Holy Spirit—are still praying. According to Romans 8:26 (ESV), *"Likewise the Spirit helps us in our weakness. For we do not know what to pray for as we ought, but the Spirit himself intercedes for us with groanings too deep for words."* Because the nature of Christ is intercessory, we are to be the change agents in the earth, interceding for things around us and beyond!

Paul

> Philippians 1:19 (ESV)
> *"Yes, and I will rejoice, for I know that through your prayers and the help of the Spirit of Jesus Christ this will turn out for my deliverance."*

The apostle Paul was well aware of the power of intercession. Paul first assured the Philippian church of the strides that preaching the gospel had made. Paul was assured that the prayers of the righteous avail much and that God answers those who cry out to him. Paul proclaimed the prayers of the saints to be something that has the power to free even himself from a situation. Intercession is not merely begging; it has a liberating force that sets people free, both naturally and spiritually. Not only did Paul attribute deliverance to intercession, but he also associated intercession to expansion and the opening up of regions that had previously been closed. The furthering of the gospel is directly connected to the prayers of the saints. Can you imagine the doors that will open for itinerant ministers if people begin to pray that doors be opened? Heaven desires to send forth preachers, but there has been a hold and it lies in the mouth of the intercessors.

Colossians 4:2-4 (ESV)

"Continue steadfastly in prayer, being watchful in it with thanksgiving. At the same time, pray also for us, that God may open to us a door for the word, to declare the mystery of Christ, on account of which I am in prison."

Conclusion

Intercession is something we all can improve in. God is raising up persistent intercessors who know how to pray the will of God in the earth so that we can see transformation take place in our communities. A great tool to put in your toolkit is Isaiah 62:6-7 (ESV), which exclaims, *"On your walls, O Jerusalem, I have set watchmen; all the day and all the night they shall never be silent. You who put the Lord in remembrance, take no rest, and give him no rest until he establishes Jerusalem and makes it a praise in the earth."* This verse reveals that intercessors do not have days off. Taking a day off can completely derail the trajectory of someone's life. Is it that serious? Yes! As a prophet, you must learn how to stand in the gap and see GOD in every situation. Having this lens will prepare you for smooth and pure prophetic function.

Our next stop is a very important one. Before we get into the making of a prophet, we must see the diet that is required of all prophets: consecration!

MINISTERS UNTO THE LORD

Consecration has almost become a curse word to the 21st century church. I can remember growing up in a church where there was always a friendly reminder that God's people were set apart from the rest of the world. Those who served God and served the people were even set apart from the rest of the chosen ones. Consider the shadow of the tabernacle of meeting. In this model, there were three phases: the outer court, the inner court, and the most holy place. As the early Israelites proceeded from one phase to the next, there were different standards or requirements as to who could enter. The closer you came to the most holy place, the more consecrated the individuals who entered were required to be. The most holy place was reserved for those who were Levites, the priests. In the most holy place, one important item was the ark of the covenant, which symbolizes the presence of God. When Jesus died the veil was ripped. This ripped the bloodline privilege from being exclusive to Levi's generations and opened it up for all of Israel and Gentiles alike. A working definition of consecration means to be set apart for God's use. Consecration is necessary. In the Old Testament, circumcision was a physical sign of Israel's covenant with God. Thankfully, this physical sign is not needed today as we all have access to this wonderful relationship with our Lord and Savior. In addition, there is internal wiring that opens the door to new heights and new realms in the spirit when an individual has been set apart by God.

The prophet's office is an ascension gift. Christ ascended and passed out offices—apostles, prophets, pastors, and teachers (Ephesians 4:11). Consequently, there is a need for prophets to ascend beyond this earthly realm in order to fulfill this office. Consider Psalms 24:1-3 (ESV), which states, "*The earth is the LORD'S and the fullness thereof, the world and those who dwell therein, for he has founded it upon the seas and established it upon the rivers. Who shall ascend the hill of the LORD? And who shall stand in his holy place? He who has clean hands and a pure heart, who does not lift up his soul to what is false and does not swear deceitfully.*" These verses give us so much clarity about the importance of becoming an individual who not only bring heaven down to earth, but also one who is consecrated enough to go up into the hill or mountain of the Lord.

Most prophets in the Bible can be seen functioning from the mountain. The mountain is the highest peak in the land and is not easily moved. This geographic formation is created by shifts in tectonic plates. Likewise, prophets are formed through shifts and sudden movements in life. Those who ascend to the mountain of God have the sight to see everything below them. Mountains also have a different atmosphere and climate. Prophets who dare to be mountainous learn how to breathe, even in hard places. Prophets are sustained by the voice of God and not by natural elements. Lastly, those who dare to function from the mountain do not succumb to the demonic high places; instead, they tear them down. It is on the mountain that demonic opposition is addressed, wars are won, destinies are revealed, provision is made, and culture is reclaimed for the Kingdom of God.

Consecration has two requirements: clean hands and a pure heart! The consecrated life requires clean hands. This call in the prophetic requires people who are willing to serve, yet they must do so with clean hands. Imagine being at a restaurant and a waiter brings your food but his hands are all dirty. Or imagine that you are in the bathroom and someone comes out from the stall and immediately walks out the door, completely bypassing the sink. That individual is to be shunned because of their uncleanliness. Likewise, ministering with dirty hands will taint the oil, attract flies, and cause glory to evade an individual. Serving with dirty hands will also cause things in the church and various sectors to become contaminated. Consequently, these individuals minister with no weight, have no heavenly back up, and constantly mope around in valleys and squander in caves. We have experienced enough of that in Christendom. This sets a precedent for emerging prophetic voices that this is the standard and that you can do whatever you desire. The devil is a liar! We are called to be separate. Consecration is a spiritual decision to separate from familiarity and the culture of this world. When an individual ascends, glory is the new normal for those who dare to live at the hill of the Lord. Bringing glory becomes easy. Later I will go into more detail, but for now, just remember that the heart is connected to meditation. Prophets who are lovers of the Word are generally people who live clean and pure lives. Later in Psalms, the prophet David tells us what to do with the word. The word must be hidden in the heart and not in the head (Psalm 119:11). Hiding the word in your head will lead to legalism and a lack of intimacy.

Consider Abraham in Genesis 22:1-5. God had given Abraham instructions to go to the land of Moriah to prepare for a sacrifice on one of the mountains. This is very insightful because God asked

Abraham to sacrifice the very thing that he had promised him: his son Isaac. Naturally, this would be a hard task. Supernaturally, this was nothing for Abraham. It was on this mountain that Abraham understood the power of ascension and consecration. Abraham could not get to this mountain by sticking with the culture or the people. It was only him and the sacrifice.

Consecration reveals that there must be a separation. Networks shift, partnerships shift, and circles shift in order for us to see and experience God. Abraham left his servants with the asses at the foot of the mountain. This lesson uncovers the necessity of being separated from people. You cannot lead people without first ascending. Releasing prophetic words is hard when an individual has not ascended. Further, consecration gives an individual authority. It shows the people who are connected to you that heaven backs you up and that you are relentless when it comes to pleasing God. Abraham's separation from anything that would hinder or slow him down allowed angelic visitation, provision, and divine intervention.

Peter calls us a royal priesthood (1 Peter 2:9), a chosen generation. This is interesting because some people believe the priesthood died in the Old Testament where the veil created and called a family unto priesthood. However, Jesus' death drafted us all unto this holy, consecrated call. Holy people are responsible for holy things! Ezekiel shows us that there are two types of people: there are priests who minister to people and there are priests who are minister unto the Lord. Now, there is a big difference between these two groups: one is called to serve people, but they cannot get close to God. The other serves God and minister unto the Lord.

Ezekiel 44:10-14 (ESV)

"But the Levites who went far from me, going astray from me after their idols when Israel went astray, shall bear their punishment. They shall be ministers in my sanctuary, having oversight at the gates of the temple and ministering in the temple. They shall slaughter the burnt offering and the sacrifice for the people, and they shall stand before the people, to minister to them. Because they ministered to them before their idols and became a stumbling block of iniquity to the house of Israel, therefore I have sworn concerning them, declares the Lord God, and they shall bear their punishment. They shall not come near to me, to serve me as priest, nor come near any of my holy things and the things that are most holy, but they shall bear their shame and the abominations that they have committed. Yet I will appoint them to keep charge of the temple, to do all its service and all that is to be done in it."

Ezekiel 44:15 (ESV)

"But the Levitical priests, the sons of Zadok, who kept the charge of my sanctuary when the people of Israel went astray from me, shall come near to me to minister to me. And they shall stand before me to offer me the fat and the blood, declares the Lord God. They shall enter my sanctuary, and they shall approach my table, to minister to me, and they shall keep my charge."

NOTICE that the sons of Zadok received the presence of God as their reward. They were able to draw near because they were consistently consecrated. They were holy when it counted. The other priests still kept their calling and continued to be recognized; however, their reward was with the people. They got to do all of the busy work. Individuals who can sin and serve people reveal their reward and their heart. I remember growing up in ministry when the Lord would call me into days of consecration. I would go weeks fasting and praying. This was to purify me. It was the key that gave me access to enter into the places that very few wanted to go. My desire was not for people but for God. When Christ is your focus, you cannot go days and hours without ministering unto the Lord. Ministering to people is people-focused; you can do that without an unction. There is no difference between people who minister to people and any other organization that gives to the poor or needy. It is a glorified organization.

Ministering to God, however, is God-focused and requires a special degree of holiness. Ministering to God is also a ministry of intercession and is life changing not only for that individual, but for those connected to them. Ministers unto the Lord get to experience the good life – walking with God in the cool of the day. This is and has always been the plan of God in dealing with humanity. It takes men and women to come out of the fallen state. A fallen state is one that is consumed with conversations with others and not with God. Never forget, consecration open doors and filthiness closes them.

Ezekiel 44:10 shows us that idolizations are hindrances to our relationships with Christ. These things stand in the way and keep us from drawing close to God. It is indeed a matter of the heart and a matter of the mind. Please realize that ministerial idolization is a demon in its own right. I remember growing and maturing in the prophetic. I was young, probably around 7 or 8, releasing prophetic words to adults. Growing up, there was a hyper-focus on pulpit ministry and an introduction to ministry online via YouTube. God protected me and often corrected me from this idol as my desire to please men was a problem. There were times I was encouraged to start uploading videos of myself preaching. God hijacked me and gave me a firm no. I was simply not ready, and my heart had yet to be circumcised. A desire to be famous and church famous was quickly dealt with. Oftentimes individuals can perform and minister in the sanctuary while their private lives are hanging on by a thread. God is raising up pure sons and daughters who have not and will not be influenced by the noise of the crowd but will strictly be moved by the cloud. When that is the birthing place of ministry, an individual is built to last.

The prophet David understood that consecration was a necessity. A lack of it can prevent an individual from experiencing their best life, one that is close and intimate with the Lord. Psalms 19:13-14 (ESV) says, *"Keep back your servant also from presumptuous sins; let them not have dominion over me! Then I shall be blameless, and innocent of great transgression. Let the words of my mouth and the meditation of my heart be acceptable in your sight, O LORD, my rock and my redeemer."* David's cry was to ensure that his mouth and his heart were clean before the Lord. Those are very important organs which carry great significance in prophetic ministry.

The heart is an organ that is symbolic of the soul realm: will, intellect, and emotions. Everything flows from the heart. Proverbs 4:23 (ESV) tells us to *"Keep your heart with all vigilance, for from it flow the springs of life."* God has used humans in the earth for prophetic words quite extensively. Humans talk to humans. The redemption and reconciliatory power of God is clothed in man. Even God had to become man to save man.

Consequently, when God calls forth a prophet or prophetic vessel, things must flow through three realms of their being: spirit, soul, and body. The word is received in the spirit, processed through the heart (soul), and spoken in the flesh (mouth). Now this is extremely important for people to understand. The word is pure when it hits the spirit. If the word becomes twisted or contorted, this usually happens in the second phase (soul). A bad soul will produce a bad word, even when the word is good and redemptive in nature. David taught us the power of consecration. It comes from the heart's posture. Examine the verse, Psalms 139:34-24(ESV), which says, *"Search me, O God, and know my heart! Try me and know my thoughts! And see if there be any grievous way in me, and lead me in the way everlasting!"* All prophetic people must understand that there is no need to be a public success while failing in private. David was clear that God is the one that searches the heart and that requires intimacy. Imagine going into heart surgery but the doctor is telling you that he is going to do it standing 20 feet away using other people and other objects to touch you. That would be simply unacceptable. Consecration requires and gives birth to true intimacy with God.

Consecration will separate an individual from the culture of the world. All prophets must assess and evaluate their lives. Ultimately, it is not only what you are eating, but it is what is eating you! Daniel understood that he could not eat and destroy demonic systems without undergoing a change in his diet. Remember, you are called to use your mouth to prophesy! Daniel refused to eat of the king's delicacies, and it proved to give birth to supernatural intelligence (Daniel 1:5-16). In addition, John the Baptist was prophesying in the desert while wearing very distinct attire and eating wild locust and honey. The very thing that was called to frustrate the harvest and plague God's children, John came away eating it! Prophetic individuals are only as potent as their consecration. There must be a distinction and a separation. God cannot use you to combat Babylon if you are involved in the culture of Babylon. All prophets had to be separated from the culture of men and sin before going forth into their calling.

In Romans 12:1-2, Paul writes, *"I appeal to you therefore, brothers, by the mercies of God, to present your bodies as a living sacrifice, holy and acceptable to God, which is your spiritual worship. Do not be conformed to this world, but be transformed by the renewal of your mind, that by testing you may discern what is the will of God, what is good and acceptable and perfect."* One of the things that really struck me while reading this verse is the fact that Paul had to beg or urge the believers to do something that should be common sense. However, I get it. Culture can impact and change individuals. Even when people are newly saved, a cycle of lukewarm

Christians can be perpetuated if they are trained and paired with people who are not truly sold out for Jesus. Paul said for us to become a "living sacrifice."

In order to live, we must die. Death is a beautiful thing because it guarantees partnership with our maker. Isaiah 6:1 (ESV) says *"In the year that King Uzziah died I saw the Lord sitting upon a throne, high and lifted up; and the train of his robe filled the temple."* Death will cause individuals to see and experience the glory realm of God! Ask yourself the following questions. Which personal relationships in your life need to die? Which idol needs to die? What throne is standing in the way of you seeing and experiencing God?

Conformity to the world or the spirit of this age will hinder individuals from being set apart for the master's use. This world will pollute your heart and cause the filter of your prophetic to be dingy. I don't know about you, but I detest things that have lost their color or flavor. The lack of consecration impacts people's willingness to receive and ultimately shuts doors. The only people who love to receive words from unclean prophets are people who are unclean themselves. Consider how many sick Christians we have today because they received a dirty word from a dirty prophet. May prophets arise that are pure, holy, consecrated, and drenched in Glory!

Apostle Paul urged the church to be transformed through mind renewal. This is critically important.

Being saved with an old mind is a horrible issue. As believers, we must access the mind of Christ. 1 Corinthians 2:16 (ESV) asks us, *"For who has understood the mind of the Lord so as to instruct him?"* But we have the mind of Christ. We must utilize and function from a different mindset, not the carnal mind. A mind is a terrible thing to waste. We are supernatural beings that have been renewed, thus, we should be renewed in the spirit of our minds. Paul discussed this issue with the church of Ephesus. There must be a difference between the clean and the unclean. Ephesians 4:20 (ESV) states, *"But that is not the way you learned Christ! — assuming that you have heard about him and were taught in him, as the truth is in Jesus, to put off your old self, which belongs to your former manner of life and is corrupt through deceitful desires, and to be renewed in the spirit of your minds, and to put on the new self, created after the likeness of God in true righteousness and holiness."*

The latter clause of Romans 12:2 explains the power of consecration and how it will help us to function as supernatural agents in a natural world. It states, *"that by testing you may discern what is the will of God, what is good and acceptable and perfect."* The lack of consecration will prohibit an individual from discerning the will of God and what is acceptable and perfect. Have you ever wondered how prophets of God can get it so wrong? It often comes down to a lack of renewal and transformation. Prophets have bad days and bad seasons where everything is perceived and missed because they have lacked the ability to discern.

If I was the devil and I wanted to corrupt a generation of true prophets, I would not get them to openly denounce Christ and go astray; I would simply pervert their gift. A bad prophetic gift is better used in the hands of the devil than a witch or blatant devil worshipper. Why? Because most true prophets have influence in the Kingdom of light. When they function in place but constantly spew off words that steer people into wrong destines, it can set the church back decades. That is why it is important and necessary to be renewed so that you will not be used as an instrument of unrighteousness. It is of utmost importance that prophets listen and discern more than they speak. I am not advocating for the devil, but we must think like the devil and see how he is taking advantage of individuals who are supposed to be walking with the Lord.

Abraham

Genesis 12:1 (ESV)

"Now the Lord said to Abram, 'Go from your country and your kindred and your father's house to the land that I will show you.'"

Abraham's call was birthed out of separation. God moved him from the culture of his family and initiated him into prophetic process. Separation must be done intentionally. There are days that are coming when people will proclaim, "here come the prophets" because they look differently, activate heavenly realms, and carry the counsel of God.

Joshua

Joshua 3:5 (ESV)

"Then Joshua said to the people, 'Consecrate yourselves, for tomorrow the Lord will do wonders among you.' And Joshua said to the priests, 'Take up the ark of the covenant and pass on before the people.' So they took up the ark of the covenant and went before the people."

Joshua was called to lead the children of Israel. He gave the people the command of consecration. This lets us know that when you are in moments of transition—whether it is into another office, city, region, or territory—there should always be consecration! This creates heavenly steps and opens up a realm of wonders. The glory dimension is ushered in through consecration. Notice that Joshua gave instructions to the priests next concerning the ark of the covenant.

There is no consecration if God is not the focus. I remember "fasting" from social media. While I abstained from this, I did not fast and spent very few hours praying. God told me that what I was doing was neither a fast nor consecration. Fasts and consecrations are days of intentionally seeking God, not just abstinence from various activities.

Isaiah

Isaiah 6:1-7 (ESV)

"In the year that King Uzziah died I saw the Lord sitting upon a throne, high and lifted up; and the train of his robe filled the temple. Above him stood the seraphim. Each had six wings: with two he covered his face, and with two he covered his feet, and with two he flew. And one called to another and said: 'Holy, holy, holy is the Lord of hosts; the whole earth is full of his glory!' And the foundations of the thresholds shook at the voice of him who called, and the house was filled with smoke. And I said: 'Woe is me! For I am lost; for I am a man of unclean lips, and I dwell in the midst of a people of unclean lips; for my eyes have seen the King, the Lord of hosts!' Then one of the seraphim flew to me, having in his hand a burning coal that he had taken with tongs from the altar. And he touched my mouth and said: 'Behold, this has

touched your lips; your guilt is taken away, and your sin atoned for."'

It took death for Isaiah to be ushered into a Godly encounter. Oftentimes we allow people to stand in the way of us encountering God. People cannot see God because their focus is on a physical person. When idols die, God can stand up! Isaiah saw God and was able to accept the call to minister. Notice that his release and initiation into prophetic ministry started with a clean mouth. This is essential! God consecrated him before he released him. If you stay in a posture to be cleaned, you will be sustained for the rest of your prophetic journey.

Joel

Joel 1:13-14 (ESV)

"Put on sackcloth and lament, O priests; wail, O ministers of the altar. Go in, pass the night in sackcloth, O ministers of my God! Because grain offering and drink offering are withheld from the house of your God. Consecrate a fast; call a solemn assembly. Gather the elders and all the inhabitants of the land to the house of the Lord your God, and cry out to the Lord."

. . .

JOEL CALLED for a fast because there were offerings that were being withheld. Notice that a bad heart will impact all areas in the life of a believer. A little filth will defile the whole temple. Be the generation that cries out to God each day!

Conclusion

Consecration is not the last thing that an individual does to prepare; it is the first thing. It should predate all other forms of servitude for the Lord. I have noticed in my personal walk with Christ that if I struggled in the area of consecration, I struggled with manifesting the Kingdom and hearing God precisely. As you read this book, you have been charged to be different and to be set apart. No more "bad or off days;" you are moving into glory days. The next chapter will open up encounters as we delve into the process of prophets. We boarded the train at consecration; the next stop is Desert Storm.

4

OPERATION DESERT STORM: HOW GOD PREPARES PROPHETS

P rophets are instruments in the earth. They are not normal civilians or normal Christians. Prophets should be mature as this realm is not for babes in Christ. According to Ephesians 2:20, Prophets are a foundational office. If the church is built on something that is flaky, malnourished, and incompetent, those who stand on it will be in danger. Some of the turmoil that has existed nationally and even internationally has occurred because there have been casual movements in and out of the office of the prophet. This has caused reproach in the church concerning the authenticity of this office. No one should just assume the office of the prophet. Doing so will warrant all of the warfare assigned to that ministry. Leaders need to understand that this is one of the most sought after, demonically infiltrated areas.

Through the prophetic, churches are directed, cities are restructured, and lives and destinies are shifted. Demon powers often try to establish demonic sleeper cells in order to create and foster demonic agendas in the earth.

The prophetic is in dire need of evaluative systems that can be used to ensure that those who enter the office are indeed sent by God and have the necessary character and processing to uphold them. A bad prophet can cause post-traumatic stress disorder (PTSD) to recipients of their ministry and make individuals shun what should be prioritized. The more I think about my own prophetic process, the more I realize that this is truly not a two-year or three-year process. It started well before I heard "you are called as a prophet." Most of the time, an individual will conclude that their journey began way before an announcement was ever made.

Growing up, I was always different. Even saying that is an understatement. Wired with the prophet's spirit, I functioned in life quite differently than my brothers, sisters, and peers. The prophet's spirit is the internal wiring carrying certain abilities, attributes, and make-up that will allow someone to walk in this office with grace. Many people who enter into it either prematurely or without the call of heaven are crushed by the office because they lack the grace to sustain it. In other words, instead of walking in the office, the office walks on them. Such individuals were never God's prophets; they were man's prophet. God equips this special branch and carries them through what I like to call "Desert Storm." This is similar to military boot camp and can happen over a series of years where God reprograms the prophetic vessel to understand the culture and domain of heaven.

Desert Storm is just what it sounds like: a storm that exists in an uncommon environment. Desert Storm is heaven's boot camp for prophetic individuals. This is the place where the prophet must learn how to adapt to an environment that may be different than their upbringing. These next few chapters are designed to give you a greater understanding of God's basic training program for prophets. The quality and output of our prophets in the church will shift when our expectations of them increase. Although there is no cookie cutter process for prophets, you will most likely find yourself transitioning through these three phases.

Basic Training

One of the first things military prospects must do is take what is known as the Armed Services Vocational Aptitude Battery Test (ASVAB). This aptitude test is given before an individual is sent to basic training and is designed to measure strengths, potential, and fundamental understanding. God prepares his prophets through life circumstances that teach and enable them to understand the fundamentals of the church as well as the fundamentals of life. We see so many examples in scripture of God taking prophets and calling them unto himself. This call is to separate and cleanse them from the culture of the world. Every prophet must be willing to be separated from familiarity and become acquainted with the nature and voice of God. No one calling themselves a prophet or prophetic voice should struggle with hearing His voice. It is too late to be "taught" after you have already stepped into the office. You can refine your hearing and learn more about your calling but knowing the voice of the Lord should not be an issue for someone who is already growing in the prophetic. In all actuality, this should be a norm for all Christians. John 10:27 (ESV) states, *"My sheep hear my voice, and I know them, and they follow me."* Below I will give you a few nuggets on how to pass through this stage with flying colors: be willing to come out of familiar environments, change your diet, increase your stamina, drop excess baggage, dress in humility, follow instructions, and walk in synchronization.

When individuals are being trained, they are carried into training environments. My wife, who is a military veteran, had to be uprooted from rural North Carolina, and travel to Chicago, Illinois, where she was stationed for several months. During this period of her life, she had to be willing to come out of familiar environments with the understanding that growth would be inevitable once she gave a "yes" to being uncomfortable. I liken this to the stage in my own life where I was raised in a Free Will Baptist church. This place was odd, weird, and unsettling. I did not choose my training ground or placement, God did. It was unconventional for most prophets, but it was here that I learned the fundamentals of sustainability. Frequently, people think that prophetic training happens in heightened prophetic atmospheres. However, while God structures some individuals in more formal environments, others are thrust into unconventional and unorthodox training sites. There are more prophets being trained in unconventional environments than those birthed from institutions. However, we now have models in which the institution of the Church exists to help prepare for the next world changes through the use of prophetic schools and training.

Being detoxed from worldly and churchy culture is important. All prophetic beings must understand that their lives are in the hand of God's voice. Matthew 4:4 (ESV) speaks of Jesus responding to Satan, *"It is written, 'Man shall not live by bread alone, but by every word that comes from the mouth of God."* Those who grew up in church occasionally have an unhealthy view of leaders. People are trained that the only way to get to Jesus is to go through a middle-man: the pastor. This unhealthy communication hierarchy must be broken off of prophetic vessels. If prophets desire to grow and move in God, they must discover the voice of God for themselves, otherwise, they could easily be driven into a vicious cycle of Simon says. As with all 5-fold ministry gifts, the prophet's mandate is bigger than the institution of the church. It is called to extend into all realms of society. Through boot camp, the prophet is recalibrated to function in God's divine order where private worship and relationship have precedence over corporate worship and servitude. Without the breaking of familiarity, a prophet could easily go rogue and become the people's puppet instead of God's prophet. Many prophets have to be removed from family and familiar environments in order to fully step into a deeper level of responsibility.

This new environment and uncomfortable place require a new diet. The internal system of prophets is different. We do not eat what others eat. Our first and foremost portion is the word of God. Prophets are and should be people of the word. It is impossible to know the "Rhema" (spoken word of God) without the "Logos" (written word of God). I can recall many experiences during my basic training where there was such a hunger inside of me to dig into the word. There were moments where I felt that God had me as an Ezekiel type, and I had to literally eat the word. These were long days of study, not just to become wordy but to become more like Jesus. The word used to, and still does, melt my heart as I long to retain information and be transformed by the Holy Spirit stepping into my room. This diet was all I needed. My meat was literally to do the will of God (John 4:34).

These were also the times where God used this training to trim the excess weight from my life. It was my word diet that caused sin and weights to fall off. It was not a 5-step program; it was the power of the presence of God. During these boot camp experiences, God is there every step of the way, preparing your meals, and letting you know that even though some things may be bitter, it is going to make you better. As a trainee, you do not choose the meal. You do not eat what you want; you eat what God gives you. Meal prep is in the hands of God. The word will challenge you, keep your attitude under subjection, and help you walk in the fruit of the Spirit. I have found out through experience that the prophets who have gone astray or who do not display the character of God have all gone AWOL (Absent With Out Leave) during "chow time."

So many movies depict basic training as a time where a senior officer is hollering or screaming at the privates or junior officers. Usually, these moments occur because a private or trainee decided to be a rebel and step out of line, therefore failing to measure up and meet expectations. Trainees are literally engrafted into a new normal. It is during basic training that God deals with the prophet's pride. There is nothing worse than a haughty prophetic vessel. God takes these moments to crush every image and sense of entitlement that the prophet has put on the shelf as a trophy. Pride is crushed through basic training because it requires team effort and collaboration. These moments are not individualized moments; they are team moments. Everything that the prophet goes through is for the maturation of the Body of Christ. Notice that there is no individualization for trainees. They go into basic training and must all follow the same instructions. It is here that prophets learn that they are not above the law. Although uniquely gifted, they are camouflaged in the unit. The peacock spirit must be intentionally given up so that humility, servitude, and comradery can be displayed. The Bible tells us that *"God resists the proud and gives more grace to the humble"* (1 Peter 5:5, ESV). There is a measure of prophetic faith and unique spiritual gifts that are given to each individual according to the grace of God. Grace, faith, and the prophetic are all tied together!

It is also on this level that character, synchronization, and stamina are birthed in prophetic vessels. Character flaws are things that are typically handled in the first stages of basic training. These are the times where God deals privately with individuals before sending them forth into the public. Long gone are the days where prophetic individuals are successful publicly but failures privately. I have come to the conclusion that bad sons are generally bad in whatever area they serve. Basic training deals with wayward and misaligned behaviors, attitudes, and motives. Consider the land of Midian that Moses fled to.

Exodus 2:15 (ESV)

"When Pharaoh heard of it, he sought to kill Moses. But Moses fled from Pharaoh and stayed in the land of Midian. And he sat down by a well."

Exodus 3:1-5 (ESV)

"Now Moses was keeping the flock of his father-in-law, Jethro, the priest of Midian, and he led his flock to the west side of the wilderness and came to Horeb, the mountain of God. And the angel of the Lord appeared to him in a flame of fire out of the midst of a bush. He looked, and behold, the bush was burning, yet it was not consumed. And Moses said, 'I will turn aside to see this great sight, why the bush is not burned.' When the Lord saw that he turned aside to see, God called to him out of the bush, 'Moses, Moses!' And he said, 'Here I am.' Then he said, 'Do not come near; take your sandals off your feet, for the place on which you are standing is holy ground.'"

MOSES' training was in the wilderness, away from his normal environment. The first encounter that he had with God was a command to take off his sandals. In the Bible, feet represent ministry and mobility. Moses was told to release all that he thought he knew and be naked before the Lord. His sandals were a physical sign of every place he had previously stepped. This was a time of true encounter with God, one that required new steps and new character. Egypt did not need the old Moses, Ramses' son; Egypt needed the prophet, God's deliverer. That required a character change and an encounter with God!

Synchronization is the programming of basic training. If you have seen or participated in any graduation ceremony, you know that it is a time of uniformity. Everyone is walking in synchronization and following the instructions of those who are superior. The prophetic grace, although powerful and distinct, is still under the thumb of leadership and open to scrutiny and review. Checks and balances are essential to the longevity of any institution. This uniformity ensures proper linkage and connection to the body of Christ. It is through basic training that prophets understand that they do not exist on their own. There is an understanding that this office is housed inside of the Kingdom and functions as an interdependent agency. Furthermore, a great deal of stamina is needed in the prophetic. Prophetic individuals must learn how to build their muscles and run the race with endurance. The devil attempts to burn prophets out by preoccupying them with the cares of life.

The basic training of prophets is integral to their development and influence. Without this, prophets are very immature and lack the necessary potency to increase in stature and influence. This preparatory period in a prophet's life helps to propel them into prominent places of influence so that they can share counsel of the Lord. God longs to use prophetic individuals, placing them in various sectors of society beyond the church to influence the world at-large. However, these individuals must successfully pass the basic training of prophets. The prophets below have unique experiences in which their gifts and character passed through preparatory phases. This is the initiation process for all prophets. Make note that all prophets are not the same. They do not have the exact same basic training programs, yet they all went through preparation and were ultimately successful.

Abraham

Genesis 12:1-3 (ESV)

"Now the Lord said to Abram, 'Go from your country and your kindred and your father's house to the land that I will show you. And I will make of you a great

nation, and I will bless you and make your name great,
so that you will be a blessing. I will bless those who bless
you, and him who dishonors you I will curse, and in you
all the families of the earth shall be blessed."'

Abraham had to walk in the land of unfamiliarity. There's no doubt that this was a challenging mandate, but it proved to be one that not only preserved Abraham but also gave way to a prophetic promise! Abraham had to be daring and had to separate in order to receive the promise. This was his basic training. Notice when you read the story of Abraham, God never gave him multiple prophetic words at one time. He received them almost like a rabbit trail. Once he ate one word and followed through with it, God would give him another. Basic training is not meant to scare you but to challenge you and to determine what you will prioritize over God. Hopefully, your answer is nothing! Just as Abraham was stuck in the land and the house of his father, God challenged him to let go of all of that so he could receive the promises of God. In exchange, he received more following God than he would have had he stayed amongst family.

Elisha

1 Kings 19:19-21 (ESV)

> "So he departed from there and found Elisha the son
> of Shaphat, who was plowing with twelve yoke of oxen
> in front of him, and he was with the twelfth. Elijah
> passed by him and cast his cloak upon him. And he left
> the oxen and ran after Elijah and said, 'Let me kiss my
> father and my mother, and then I will follow you.' And
> he said to him, 'Go back again, for what have I done to
> you?' And he returned from following him and took the
> yoke of oxen and sacrificed them and boiled their flesh
> with the yokes of the oxen and gave it to the people, and
> they ate. Then he arose and went after Elijah and
> assisted him."

Elisha's basic training was more formal. Whereas Abraham had to learn on his own, Elisha was able to see a spiritual example by walking closely with his prophetic father. Elisha's natural father was still alive, yet he realized that what he needed was locked inside of another man. His basic training was difficult, and he left home, not in a negative way but in a respectable way. Elisha showed us that while you may be on a prophetic course, how you leave a place will determine how you enter a new season. He fulfilled his obligations at home where he had sacrificed to feed the people. He left a pastoral mandate feeding people to fulfill a prophetic call of serving his spiritual father. Also, it is important to consider the implications of the fact that Elisha was working before he was called to take a prophetic mandate. I like to think that Elisha was chosen because he was not a lazy individual. Growing up, I noticed that some people refuse to serve if they feel as though they are not doing something extravagant for the Kingdom. Elisha was working, doing the hard work stirring yokes of oxen. Those years of serving were a silent season for Elisha. The only conversing that you really notice with him was his obedience and tenuous spirit to never leave his man of God. Having that grace to serve opened a realm of prophetic lineage that guaranteed his success and longevity.

Joseph

Genesis 37:1-4 (ESV)

"Jacob lived in the land of his father's sojournings, in the land of Canaan. These are the generations of Jacob. Joseph, being seventeen years old, was pasturing the flock with his brothers. He was a boy with the sons of Bilhah and Zilpah, his father's wives. And Joseph brought a bad report of them to their father. Now Israel loved Joseph more than any other of his sons, because he was the son of his old age. And he made him a robe of many colors. But when his brothers saw that their father loved him more than all his brothers, they hated him and could not speak peacefully to him."

Genesis 37:9-11 (ESV)

"Then he dreamed another dream and told it to his brothers and said, 'Behold, I have dreamed another dream. Behold, the sun, the moon, and eleven stars were bowing down to me.' But when he told it to his father and to his brothers, his father rebuked him and said to him, 'What is this dream that you have dreamed? Shall I and your mother and your brothers indeed come to bow ourselves to the ground before you?' And his brothers were jealous of him, but his father kept the saying in mind."

Joseph's prophetic pull began much earlier than Abraham and Elisha's did. Joseph was forced into boot camp as a young boy when he started having dreams. His prophetic eyes were opened much earlier and his initiation into the prophetic was quite different. Joseph was favored by his father and the pompous prophetic words he received from God sent him into a more intense training program. I love the story of Joseph, but God had to humble the young lad and teach him prophetic etiquette and timing. Notice that he already had a coat of many colors. I can almost see him right now strutting with his fancy coat. His out of timing prophetic words landed him right into the pit where he was separated to be elevated. It was during those moments that Joseph had to trust in God! It was during those moments that Joseph had to realize that the prophetic is not just something that can elevate you; it is something that can save you and others. First, he had to be introduced to the jail cell of the prophetic. No one cared about his gift, sight, or dreams. It was just him and God! This time humbled Joseph and when we see him in the next chapter, we see how God refined his spiritual sight and delivery.

Elijah

1 Kings 17:2-7 (ESV)

"And the word of the Lord came to him: 'Depart from here and turn eastward and hide yourself by the brook Cherith, which is east of the Jordan. You shall drink from the brook, and I have commanded the ravens to feed you there.' So he went and did according to the word of the Lord. He went and lived by the brook Cherith that is east of the Jordan. And the ravens brought him bread and meat in the morning, and bread and meat in the evening, and he drank from the brook. And after a while the brook dried up, because there was no rain in the land."

Elijah's personal history is not recorded. He pops up in scripture unbeknownst to the reader. The land that he is from—Tish—is also untraceable. Now, both of those statements can be a whole sermon! If you can stand before God, you can stand before anyone. Also, although there are bloodline blessings and spiritual gifts and callings resting in families, you can be called because you are in the bloodline of Christ! Elijah comes bearing the word of God and leaves after making his announcement. The fact that heaven backed his word was his passing grade. Afterward, God took him and gave him instructions. He had to learn how to live off of the word of God. God had to prepare his diet by giving him his daily instructions. Elijah leaned on every word God spoke as God led him through several obstacles, yet he continued to stick with it. After getting accustomed to being fed by ravens, God dried up the brook and sent him around other humans. Human interaction during the basic training is vital. There is nothing more frightening than a sheltered prophet; they often make the prophetic look and sound weird. For Elijah, this was a time of reliance on God. It would have been outlandish for Elijah to think he could defeat Jezebel and all of her false prophets if he did not know how to eat. Basic training taught Elijah how to trust God and how to hear God!

Ezekiel

Ezekiel 2:8-10 (ESV)

"But you, son of man, hear what I say to you. Be not

rebellious like that rebellious house; open your mouth and eat what I give you.' And when I looked, behold, a hand was stretched out to me, and behold, a scroll of a book was in it. And he spread it before me. And it had writing on the front and on the back, and there were written on it words of lamentation and mourning and woe."

Ezekiel's basic training was very intense. God had to make him tough. As prophetic individuals, there will be times where you will have to stand against the norm. But when you stand with God, He will lean the scale in your favor. His presence and instructions give you the upper hand in every situation. Another thing that Ezekiel had to learn was radical obedience. Oftentimes we wonder why God will harden or give prophetic people hard words; it is not only for the people, but it is also for the deliverer. When you can stand and deliver to rebellious people, you are on your way to being used as a mighty instrument of righteousness.

Ezekiel had to eat the scroll. His dietary disposition was in the hands of God. He did not choose what he thought was fitting but instead ate what God provided. At the basic training level, your options and choices are limited if you desire to move to the next level. Oftentimes people have arrested development because they believe they know what is best for them. At this place, Ezekiel shows us that we must blindly trust God, regardless of what our carnal mind is telling us. This sometimes seem difficult yet following God's instruction is rewarding. At the basic training level there are tears, mourning, and even experiences that are breathtaking. God had to show Ezekiel how to experience and travail with the burden of the Lord. This is intercessory in nature as Ezekiel had to understand how to pray and lament for a nation that was rebellious. This reveals that God can use any situation to raise up prophets. There will be situations in which you will be accepted and then there are situations where people do not respect the prophetic in you. Always remember that it is not personal; it is a God situation. As prophets, we must be obedient, eat the scroll, and do what we are told because at the basic training level; we have no say in what we eat, where we go, or what we do. We are completely spirit led.

Conclusion

God does not just release prophets into the world without teaching them the fundamentals of the prophetic. These foundational truths are typically learned through God's basic training program. If you are going through this right now, learn all that God has for you. Do not cheat yourself short or cut corners. If you do, you will regret it later when you find yourself lacking the vital resources and wisdom necessary for where God is sending you.

This chapter dealt with how God prepares the prophet. The next chapter will dive into how God staffs and equips prophets once they have passed basic training.

5

OPERATION DESERT STORM: HOW GOD EQUIPS PROPHETS

Prophetic ministry is not for the weary or the faint of heart. The development of your ministry will require more than one season of training. It reminds me of when I began my career as a teacher, something which was extremely challenging for me because I had to learn all of the teaching material while simultaneously learning different methods of teaching. I completed my internship and was fully ready to step into the world as a high school history teacher; however, before I was allowed to sign my first contract, I had to participate in a weeklong program called Summer Bridge. This was a required program that new teachers had to complete before being allowed to teach in the county. I completed this week of training, signed my contract, and entered the field of teaching. Upon entering this field, I had a mentor and a principal assigned to follow my development. This was an intense year. So many eyes were upon me and there were so many levels of accountability. Suddenly, after a month of teaching, they started requiring us to attend professional development events twice a week. This constant training helped me continue to develop in my field. When I became a principal, I participated in the same process. Likewise, when an individual is under prophetic apprenticeship, desert storm is not over just because they received a degree, certificate, or were recognized as a star prophet. All of the beginning knowledge and lessons are just stepping-stones for an even higher level of learning, practice, and training.

When an individual decides to shun learning, that person has welcomed dry and stale seasons to infiltrate their ministry. The apostle Paul made an important point that sums up my own tenacity in the prophetic. In 2 Corinthians 3:18 (ESV), he writes, *"And we all, with unveiled face, beholding the glory of the Lord, are being transformed into the same image from one degree of glory to another. For this comes from the Lord who is the Spirit."* There are levels to the prophetic, and it is in the glory dimension where we must be willing to undergo the process, step out of pride, and realize that once you "know" everything, you have nowhere left to go. Humility will teach you not only other realms of God but other realms in the prophetic. Mastery of the different stages of the prophetic comes through intense, stratified levels of training. Basic training will give you basic prophetic function; however, allowing God to take you to the next level and submitting to the process will afford you the ability to learn and function at a heightened level. 1 Corinthians 14:31-32 (ESV) states, *"For you can all prophesy one by one, so that all may learn and all be encouraged, and the spirits of prophets are subject to prophets."* As it relates to prophetic ministry, the apostle Paul is encouraging one-by-one prophetics. There is power when there is order in the prophetic and when people can engage and observe prophetic administration. In this atmosphere, people can learn and be encouraged from the words that prophets release.

Desert storm can be categorized into three levels: basic training, advanced individualized training (AIT), and the call of duty. AIT is the next level of prophetic training and is beyond the basic fundamentals of Christianity and the prophetic. At this level, the individual is provoked to function as a prophetic vessel and demonstrate awareness, prophetic latitude and longitude, and is graced to learn their mandate all before being officially launched into their area of prophetic expertise.

Advanced Individualized Training

AIT is totally different from basic training. The military is very strategic, and it is impossible to enter into this second phase without successfully passing the first. Unfortunately, in most instances, local churches do not have such rigid systems in place for prophets and prophetic people. There is a lot of personal responsibility required in understanding and being truthful about what phase you feel God is taking you through. Honesty will afford you the ability to gather all you can. It is important to know what God is pulling on and pulling out of you during your process. Consequently, you will have individuals who may enter into individualized prophetic training and begin to function without having passed basic training. This is dangerous and will always reap a reward of failure and perpetual trouble. As a prophetic individual, be careful and ensure that you have learned the basics of prophetic responsibility before delving into the greater and more tedious realms of the prophetic. Each level comes with an even greater responsibility than the one before it.

Journeying through AIT will afford you many opportunities to excel. This level of training is very specific. It is here that you advance beyond the elementary, generic teaching and start to become awakened to your true identity. Everyone's journey is different, and you will transition from being in a "group" to becoming an individual. Because you have been humbled under basic training, God can now separate you from the group and introduce you to like-minded prophetic individuals who have some of the same traits and delivery systems. Listening to my wife's experience in AIT revealed a myriad of benefits such as hands-on activities, individualized training, special opportunities, expert teachers at your disposal, and self-realization (identity).

During AIT, what is inside of you will come out. There are times where prophetic individuals should be intentional about pushing into their spheres of prophetic calling and mandates. As a prophetic type, David was given an opportunity to display and develop in two of his prophetic areas: warring and psalmistry. Basic training in the field prepared David to be protective, obedient, and humble. These basic moments were stepping-stones for his prophetic assignment as a prophet. Let's examine two of David's hands-on opportunities.

1 Samuel 16:21-23 (ESV)

"And David came to Saul and entered his service. And Saul loved him greatly, and he became his armor-bearer. And Saul sent to Jesse, saying, 'Let David remain in my service, for he has found favor in my sight.' And whenever the harmful spirit from God was upon Saul,

David took the lyre and played it with his hand. So Saul was refreshed and was well, and the harmful spirit departed from him."

One of the training grounds for prophetic ministers is in the realm of arts, specifically music. David's first operation in hearing God came by way of his skillful and methodical musical notes. In doing so, he not only set the atmosphere but addressed the devil and demonic entities. The prophetic is bigger than just releasing words. It involves setting atmospheres and allowing the King to step in the room. It takes prophetic ability to create the tone and lay out the red carpet for heaven to invade space. Musicians and psalmists must be intuitive in prophetic function. Prophets move in deliverance. David walked in such authority that his notes drove out demons. This shows us that prophets carry mantles that frustrates the devil. This is not just a ministry in which one just sits around and does nothing. It is confrontational and will usher in God at any cost.

Growing up, my parents began to train me to play the keys. I used to usher in the presence of God. I was not the most skillful, but it was through my playing that the prophetic anointing would crack open in the church house. Now, this was a Baptist church, so can you imagine people crying out to God and prophetic utterances being released? The ministry of music matters and is often the training ground and the launching pad for prophetic individuals. Some stay there and function as a prophetic minstrel or musician, while others leave and carry other prophetic mantles. While growing up, I also used to sing the song of the Lord. These were special moments in which God would download spontaneous lyrics in the midst of worship. This turned from singing the song of the Lord to speaking the word of the Lord. Do not despise small beginnings. Operating under the musical realm of the prophetic led David into the warring and governmental realms of the prophetic.

1 Samuel 17:32-40 (ESV)

"And David said to Saul, 'Let no man's heart fail because of him. Your servant will go and fight with this Philistine.' And Saul said to David, 'You are not able to go against this Philistine to fight with him, for you are but a youth, and he has been a man of war from his youth.' But David said to Saul, 'Your servant used to keep sheep for his father. And when there came a lion, or a bear, and took a lamb from the flock, I went after him and struck him and delivered it out of his mouth. And if he arose against me, I caught him by his beard and struck him and killed him. Your servant has struck down both lions and bears, and this uncircumcised Philistine shall be like one of them, for he has defied the armies of the living God.' And David said, 'The Lord who delivered

me from the paw of the lion and from the paw of the bear will deliver me from the hand of this Philistine.' And Saul said to David, 'Go, and the Lord be with you!' Then Saul clothed David with his armor. He put a helmet of bronze on his head and clothed him with a coat of mail, and David strapped his sword over his armor. And he tried in vain to go, for he had not tested them. Then David said to Saul, 'I cannot go with these, for I have not tested them.' So David put them off. Then he took his staff in his hand and chose five smooth stones from the brook and put them in his shepherd's pouch. His sling was in his hand, and he approached the Philistine."

The first opportunity for David to grow in his prophetic development occurred after he went through basic training. He received his certificate and badge of honor from basic training when Samuel came to anoint him as the next King (1 Samuel 16:1). His field experience— tussling over the sheep—and humility ensured his promotion from the pasture to the palace. Furthermore, his announcement alone was not good enough. There was another level of training (AIT) that he had to endure in order to have longevity and competence as both the King of Israel and as a prophet of the Most High. David is presented with an issue that only he could solve, a situation tailored specifically to help grow his prophetic mandate. No one else fit the job description and he could not wear anyone's armor.

Note here, everyone's mantle cannot be worn by you. How others flow prophetically may not be your portion or your style.

It is important during AIT that you learn YOU. This only comes from intimacy with your commander-in-chief, Jesus. Reading self-help books on the prophetic are good for general understanding; however, you must understand your own unique flow and function so that when you are presented into battle you are not weighted down with someone's armor. David had to reject Saul's recommendation. David was a prophetic warrior. This was a crash course for him to learn how to conquer the small tasks before he was out on his own fighting next level demons. Notice that Goliath was training for David. He would ultimately be released later to combat against someone who ranked higher and was stealthier than Goliath: Saul. During David's fight with Goliath, he pulled out five smooth stones representing grace and the five-fold counterattack, but in the end, used only the prophetic one. This stone was strategic and landed in the right spot on the head of Goliath (1 Samuel 17:42). One hit was all that was needed. David's stone had so much prophetic precision.

During AIT, prophetic people receive individualized training that is tailored to their unique prophetic type. Whether it involves intercession, worship, or prophetic presbytery opportunities, the prophet must learn how to maneuver under Holy Spirit in order to pass through this stage with flying colors. Further, the prophetic candidate should display and demonstrate proficiency and competence in the following areas: discipline, vulnerability, increased work ethic, and advanced spiritual fitness.

Discipline

This level of ministry is nothing to play with. It takes extreme discipline. The higher you move up in God, the less room you have for errors. You will have days when you desire to scream, quit, and run. However, you must remember who called you and how important your mandate is. Many things will come to try to throw you off of your game, but you must stick with it. Consider Jesus in Matthew 4. He was minding his business when he was approached by Satan who tried to tempt him with a variety of different things, including some from his future. Jesus had enough sense to stick with the mandate for that time. Likewise, when you are in AIT, it is not the time to try to launch out into your future if God has not instructed you to.

It is extremely vital that your flesh is under subjection. When God is increasing your influence, you can do the most damage to yourself and your reputation because people see you. It is vital to your prophetic credibility that you remember to be on your "A" game because people are watching and so is God. The worst thing that you can ever do is be a deterrent to other people and prevent them from coming into the Kingdom because of your lifestyle or because you have given them something that is off and out of season. As you enter into AIT and beyond, remember there were two instances where Moses struck the rock. The first time he received a slap on the wrist (Exodus 17). The second time, that strike locked him out of the promise land (Numbers 20). Once you progress in God, the consequences are greater.

Vulnerability

As you move into your area of expertise, it is important that humility is your friend. If there are things that you feel you need to learn before walking in the office, be brave enough to ask questions. Ask the Holy Spirit first and then ask other trusted and verified prophetic vessels. One of the blessings of humility is exaltation. God exalts and gives grace to the humble (1 Peter 5:5). There is a dimension of prophetic grace that is released when you say, "God teach me your ways." There were times even in my prophetic development that I had to ask God to teach me because there was something that I did not quite understand. As I searched the word, the Word searched me and filled me with revelation. When you are in AIT, you must understand that it will stretch you. God will break everything in you just so that he can build you back up. You must be vulnerable and willing to be trained so that God can thrust you forth in power.

This stage is almost synonymous with Elijah when he was fleeing from Jezebel. God allowed situations in his life to occur so he could understand that he was not the ONLY prophet God had. This vulnerable spot served in the character and cognitive development of prophet Elijah. He had to have assurance even in the voice of the Lord, and it was there that God gave him a future by securing his posterity in Elisha (1 Kings 19:16). Surely, you must understand that the AIT phase is created to deal with every speck in your life that is not like God. This phase is the time for mistakes, learning, and growth. During the next phase, there will be less mistakes and more prophetic function.

Work Ethic and Spiritual Fitness

In AIT, your fitness can be tested at random. It's like with physical fitness when some people have fitness splurges where they are only fit for the summer or for a specific occasion and then go back to their old patterns. AIT will shape you for an eternal prophetic journey. AIT training lasts for various timespans based on the individual's level and calling. Some people go through their journey for years, while others learn in months. Nevertheless, it is ultimately God who commissions and solidifies the call. Notice that a leader can ordain and commission. I have seen in my day many people who filled the office but never became it. It takes the oil of heaven to authorize one to become the office of the prophet—it is a person not a title.

Work ethics are of a progressive nature, and in AIT, yours should increase significantly. It may differ based on assignment, location, and calling. It is God who trains the prophet to lose all sense of rigidness and become truly prophetic. Religious mindsets are removed, and God will deliberately alternate the times that he speaks in order to help the prophet move into purpose. I remember going through my own AIT. This was not like when I was in basic. In basic, God spoke all of the time. He assured me by being there and letting me know that he had me. Words were clear, precise, and right there when I needed it. When I entered my AIT phase, God spoke but it was in a room of crowed people or in a mall at a distance. I had to learn how to locate the word of the Lord. He changed up on me quite frequently. The change was in frequency, time, scope, and depth of the prophetic. I had to quickly learn that his spontaneity kept the rust off of my gift and allowed me to always have an ear ready to hear God even in the most difficult situations.

The prophets below all went through AIT. Their

experience and length varied, yet they all eventually triumphed, therefore qualifying themselves to move to the next level.

Joseph

Ephesians 40:4-8 (ESV)

"The captain of the guard appointed Joseph to be with them, and he attended them. They continued for some time in custody. And one night they both dreamed —the cupbearer and the baker of the king of Egypt, who were confined in the prison—each his own dream, and each dream with its own interpretation. When Joseph came to them in the morning, he saw that they were troubled. So he asked Pharaoh's officers who were with him in custody in his master's house, 'Why are your faces downcast today?' They said to him, 'We have had dreams, and there is no one to interpret them.' And Joseph said to them, 'Do not interpretations belong to God? Please tell them to me.'"

Joseph went through basic training in Genesis 37 while working with his brothers and journeying through the pit. This time was a humbling experience for him and his gift. Joseph experienced prophetic trouble as his dreams and prophetic insight brought envy. His brothers were jealous and sold him which landed him in a pit, whereas his purity concerning Potiphar's wife subsequently landed him in jail. Throughout all his trouble, the hand of God was with him and on his prophetic gift. It just needed more attention and a push. Joseph experienced the pit, the palace, and then prison. The prison was Joseph's AIT training. It was here that his gift of interpretation and prophetic administration was challenged. This successful time in hearing the voice of God and being put to the test proved that he was ready for the palace again. Joseph was not caught off guard. He understood that the situation demanded prophetic insight and he pressed in immediately. AIT is a spontaneous time of prophetic delivery. It is at these times that God will put your gift on demand so that you exercise, develop, and get used to working it. Joseph's accuracy and heart posture caused him to pass through AIT and released him into another prophetic rank.

Moses

Exodus 33:12-16 (ESV)

"Moses said to the Lord, 'See, you say to me, 'Bring up this people,' but you have not let me know whom you will send with me. Yet you have said, I know you by name, and you have also found favor in my sight.' Now therefore, if I have found favor in your sight, please show

me now your ways, that I may know you in order to find favor in your sight. Consider too that this nation is your people.' And he said, 'My presence will go with you, and I will give you rest.' And he said to him, 'If your presence will not go with me, do not bring us up from here. For how shall it be known that I have found favor in your sight, I and your people? Is it not in your going with us, so that we are distinct, I and your people, from every other people on the face of the earth?'"

Moses' basic training occurred in the wilderness while detoxing from the Egyptian culture. I also believe that some of his basic training involved learning how to be radically obedient to the Father. Going back and forth with Pharaoh proved that he was ready for his next level, AIT. This level can be seen in his dealings with the people that he served. They often frustrated Moses, but as an intercessory prophet, he stood in the gap for them and upheld them. He can be seen interceding and pleading to God on their behalf. God proved to Moses that he is a gracious God, one who fulfills his promises.

The AIT level reveals the true heart of prophets. Ask yourself how you respond to trouble and adversity when people are NOT watching. Moses had a strong relationship with the Father, even when the people rejected him and did him wrong. His stance was a holy response. He handled people during this phase of his life with delicacy and intercession. He modeled for others that what he had was not something phony. His relationship and call were real and intentional. AIT brings out the best in people. It is at this place that they marry and become one with their mandate.

Daniel

Daniel 6:6-13 (ESV)

"Then they answered and said before the king, 'Daniel, who is one of the exiles from Judah, pays no attention to you, O king, or the injunction you have signed, but makes his petition three times a day.' Then the king, when he heard these words, was much distressed and set his mind to deliver Daniel. And he labored till the sun went down to rescue him. Then these men came by agreement to the king and said to the king, 'Know, O king, that it is a law of the Medes and Persians that no injunction or ordinance that the king establishes can be changed.' Then the king commanded, and Daniel was brought and cast into the den of lions. The king declared to Daniel, 'May your God, whom you serve continually, deliver you!'"

AIT is for the resilient. It is a stage of holiness that is not for those who have obedience issues. After all, obedience is a basic training matter. Daniel went through very basic trials in his life, however, his persistence elevated him to rule. Daniel was persistent in his intimacy with God. He proved in Daniel 1 and 2 that he was not going to succumb to the culture of the environment that he was in. He was going to be steadfast and prophetic in every situation. Nevertheless, because he followed orders from heaven, it landed him in a tight situation. Daniel was placed in a lion's den. His obedience granted him the opportunity and the fortitude to rest on what was designed to take him out. His prophetic ministry was on trial. He did not order this set up, AIT ordered it. This is a message to all of you who are currently in this phase: you do not order your trials, God does. When you are obedient and have a regiment of prayer and fasting set aside, you will pass with flying colors.

Rhoda and the Church

Acts 12:5;12-15 (ESV)

"So Peter was kept in prison, but earnest prayer for him was made to God by the church. -- When he realized this, he went to the house of Mary, the mother of John whose other name was Mark, where many were gathered together and were praying. And when he knocked at the door of the gateway, a servant girl named Rhoda came to answer. Recognizing Peter's voice, in her

joy she did not open the gate but ran in and reported that Peter was standing at the gate. They said to her, 'You are out of your mind.' But she kept insisting that it was so, and they kept saying, 'It is his angel!'"

Peter was locked up in prison because of persecution. The fact that the church is praying here in this scripture shows us that this is beyond the conversion or basic training level. The church is so militant in its intercession that it provokes the angelic guard to come. AIT requires discipline and stamina: the church is praying despite the current situation, and their tenacity in prayer yields a prophetic moment. The very thing they are praying for and decreeing starts to knock on the door. Rhoda is in a house full of prayer partners, yet she was awakened in her hearing faculties to discern that Peter was now knocking on the door. Nobody else heard it. AIT pulls the prophetic awareness out of you. Her discipline and faith in God yield promising results. Not only was God working in Peter, but he was also working with Rhoda.

Peter's preaching landed him in prison. This moment would be trying for any prophetic person when what was supposed to help him is seemingly hurting him. The gospel landed him in a cell. This moment could have been a crash and burn for Peter's mental state, yet Peter rested. What looked like a place of misery turned into a site that ripe for a miracle.

Peter was ushered into a realm of apostolic and prophetic function that was unprecedented in the book of Acts.

Conclusion

Desert Storm does not last forever. It is a time of self-reflection and personal advancement. The season of AIT has not been designed to crush you; it has been designed by heaven to catapult you into stronger prophetic function. The ground and the course have been designed so that you can be a functioning prophetic vessel. Every prophet goes through this phase, and some die in this stage of development because they do not want to answer the call of growth. Understanding these nuggets will help you maneuver as God calls you deeper in the prophetic. During this time, ask God what prophetic area you are called to, how you should flow, and where you are to be stationed as a prophetic vessel. The answers to these questions will help you find your grace. It will take discipline, vulnerability, a teachable spirit, stamina, and a yielded vessel to go all of the way with our Lord and Savior, Jesus the Christ.

6

OPERATION DESERT STORM: HOW GOD
SENDS PROPHETS

D esert Storm was created by God to adequately send his prophetic vessels into various sectors of society, with a special emphasis on the sending and placement of church prophets. Each stage of Desert Storm has several compartments and learning phases that will ultimately result in prophetic vessels developing the necessary skillsets and tools to ensure longevity in their individual assignments. As with the Armed Services, once basic training and AIT are complete, the real work begins.

Prophets and prophetic people are not to be released into regular society without proper supervision, accountability, and responsibility. Once released, they must continually respond to those who are over them. The Kingdom of God has structure. The days of the freelancer and lack of accountability have long been gone. Prophetic vessels respond best in environments where honor exists—honor for the leadership and honor for prophetic environments. It is imperative that your gift and training occur in places where there is respect for your calling and areas where you can use your gift. Simultaneously, you must ensure that you always maintain respect for your leader and delegated authority. Dishonor will diminish favor.

Anything that is not used will enter into the realm of abuse. I know many of you are thinking, how is this abuse? How is abuse connected to inactivity? It is called negligence. When there is a neglect of the prophetic purpose of the church, there is malnourishment, misdirection, and disregard. After the first two phases of training, prophets and prophetic people enter into a realm of jurisdiction. Spiritual jurisdiction is the legal authority given by God to make decisions. There is a place in the prophetic where God entrusts the prophet to overturn what is being done or seen. It is one thing to see it, it is another realm of authority when one can by the spirit reverse what is seen. This place is reserved for those who are indeed office prophets and those who walk with God.

While some are elevated into the office of the prophet, there are others who are elevated into other roles. God has special ways that he sends prophets. Ephesians 4:11-13 tells us, *"And he gave the apostles, the prophets, the evangelists, the shepherds and teachers, to equip the saints for the work of ministry, for building up the body of Christ, until we all attain to the unity of the faith and of the knowledge of the Son of God, to mature manhood, to the measure of the stature of the fullness of Christ."* The prophetic ministry is for the edification and unification of the body of Christ, for ministerial activity, and for revealing the knowledge of Christ. Without it, the church will lack in function and be utterly incomplete. Prophets who have passed through the basic and AIT level of preparation generally understand their mandate to build the body of Christ, whereas basic training and AIT are generally populated with people who are new to prophetic streams or people who operate under the spirit of prophesy but still need refinement in their character.

It is very important for you to know your place. There is a grace for every place that God has stationed you. Your duty assignment is not necessarily going to be your favorite place; however, you are strategically planted in the area where you are needed and where your toolset could add to the structure. For instance, there are some prophetic people who have a strong gift of intercession. Once they finish basic training and AIT, it would not be uncommon for them to be placed in an intercessory leadership role of a local church or network. Oftentimes, networks and churches fail because people are placed into positions without a resume of adequate training or God's oil over their lives. Placing a prophetic person over intercession without the proper training can easily usurp the authority of the church, turning intercession into prophetic witchcraft sessions where words are used to control the minds and the hearts of people.

This is one of the reasons that tested prophets and prophetic people should be over these functions. Consider a car: no company just takes a car and puts in on the road once it is made. It is tested long before it is ever purchased or driven by a customer. The test does not mean that the customer will never have to have a checkup or replace a part; however, it will ensure that some of the necessary components are there to ensure the safety of the individual and everyone else on board. Prophetic individuals that have surrendered and submitted to God's process can be sent and placed anywhere but will always add to the value of the church. Apostles need prophets just as much as prophets need apostles. God sends his prophetic people out of training and into combat. God sends prophets with territorial mandates and influence in the spirit of Elijah: as prophetic collaborators with overseer capabilities.

Territorial Mandates

Your placement is as important as your calling. Being in the wrong place with the right prophetic skillset is a horrible combination for a prophetic individual. There are local, regional, national, and international mandates that prophets must know in order to be effective in their placement. There is warfare attached to all of these assignments, thus, it is imperative that you know where you are placed. An out of place prophetic vessel will attract the wrong warfare, ultimately, causing that person to enter into defeated seasons. For example, an international prophet is not prepared to fight and deal with the warfare assigned to a local mandate. When you are placed in the correct environment, you will always have "home field" advantage.

The institution of the church is the command center for the body of Christ. This is very important. Being connected to a local church will bring levels of accountability, infrastructures that can assist and save your life, and a community of believers that can pour and build you up when there are seasons that seem volatile. There are times in which an individual may operate in multiple territories. For example, I function as an apostolic and prophetic leader over a church. Every church has a local mandate to serve the community that it is placed it. The church alone is a portal for heaven to rule and reign in the community. Leading this Hub and raising up prophets are my apostolic and prophetic mandates. Yet, there has been a more developed call on my life to raise up prophets on a national and international scale. Although I am respected in my local region, there is a more defined grace that God has given me nationally and internationally. There is more honor and more release at that level, so while I focus on the local and regional assignment, I cannot negate that higher mandate. Therefore, in my function, I am intentional to engage in that realm not only through prayer but also in prophetic practice.

It is very important to know and discern when there is a shift in your assignment or focus. Nehemiah 1:3-4 (ESV) states, *"And they said to me, 'The remnant there in the province who had survived the exile is in great trouble and shame. The wall of Jerusalem is broken down, and its gates are destroyed by fire.' As soon as I heard these words I sat down and wept and mourned for days, and I continued fasting and praying before the God of heaven."* Nehemiah was in a high position serving the Persian King, which was somewhat of an international placement. However, he ultimately realized that his assignment was a local, regional one. Nehemiah's focus was to build a wall for Jerusalem. Because he had a grace for this assignment, the opposition was fruitless. Nehemiah and his team had the necessary weaponry and focus to accomplish the goal.

However, there are times in which an individual's mandate may shift. David, for example, had a mandate in which his assignment and focus was local, at the familial level. Although it had a natural significance, this assignment was preparatory for his elevation and is evidenced when God shifted him from local to regional. According to 1 Samuel 17:33-35 (ESV), *"And Saul said to David, 'You are not able to go against this Philistine to fight with him, for you are but a youth, and he has been a man of war from his youth.' But David said to Saul, 'Your servant used to keep sheep for his father. And when there came a lion, or a bear, and took a lamb from the flock, I went after him and struck him and delivered it out of his mouth. And if he arose against me, I caught him by his beard and struck him and killed him.'"* David's assignment in the local house was everything he needed. Not only was it profitable for his father, the owner of the sheep, but it was also profitable and beneficial for David. When you serve a mandate, whether local or international, it will benefit you.

Influence

When God sends you forth, He will release you with a level of influence. One of the things that we have seen as a prophetic picture throughout the Old and New Testaments is that prophetic individuals are trusted in places outside of the church and other religious institutions. For so long, people have aspired to become church famous while having no authority or influence in the world. We must realize that we have a kingdom mandate and God desires to flip the world into its rightful position. God does this by raising up kingdom citizens with integrity, character, and prophetic acquisition who can then go out at direct the world.

Your prophetic mandate is only as strong as your development. The individuals that God sends will have influence because of the repertoire of skills and discipline that they that have acquired through basic and AIT. David influenced Saul, Joseph influenced Pharaoh, Elijah influenced Ahab and had the opportunity to even minister the word of the Lord. Samuel influenced Saul, Nathan had the ear of King David, Daniel had the ear of the King, and Jesus had the influence to shift and draw crowds. Without influence, no one will listen. It is essential that moments with dignitaries are not taken lightly and that there is grace and wisdom when ministering the word of the Lord.

Genesis 41:37-43 (ESV)

"This proposal pleased Pharaoh and all his servants. And Pharaoh said to his servants, 'Can we find a man like this, in whom is the Spirit of God?' Then Pharaoh said to Joseph, 'Since God has shown you all this, there is none so discerning and wise as you are. You shall be over

my house, and all my people shall order themselves as you command. Only as regards the throne will I be greater than you.' And Pharaoh said to Joseph, 'See, I have set you over all the land of Egypt.' Then Pharaoh took his signet ring from his hand and put it on Joseph's hand, and clothed him in garments of fine linen and put a gold chain about his neck. And he made him ride in his second chariot. And they called out before him, 'Bow the knee!' Thus he set him over all the land of Egypt."

JOSEPH'S prophetic ability opened way for him to rule and have access in an uncommon place. He was not from Egypt, yet he gained heavy influence and authority there. I really believe that this is the design of heaven for all prophetic and apostolic people. There are seats in the earth that are reserved for those who have prophetic wisdom and insight. Not only was this a place of dominion for Joseph, but it was a place of restoration for his family and their lineage. Instead of fighting for seats in church pulpits, there are other, bigger seats that really matter. God required Joseph to go through basic training and AIT because he was being sent to the palace. Those places prepared him for a mandate that reached beyond Egypt.

Joseph's reach was international; however, he had to go through some very weird environments first. It is amazing how God used a ransom to prepare Joseph for various territories. Imagine if prophetic people stopped complaining that people in their family do not receive them. Could it be that your reach is not local or familial? Joseph had to learn that there was a greater measure of favor beyond his local area. Basic training had to strip his coat off because there was a Pharaoh that had to put another coat on him. This coat accompanied a ring, signifying authority and covenant.

The Spirit of Elijah

Many of the prophets today want the power and gift of Elijah but do not desire to walk in his spirit. Elijah is one of the most desired prophetic types in the Old Testament. Growing up in Pentecostal circles, every prophet wanted to be like Elijah. Being sent by God into your station or zone is an honor; however, prophets must possess the spirit of Elijah. This prophet was a man of humility. Humility is absolutely needed when God has given you a prophetic mandate. There will be times when the gift will attract attention, but it must all be pointed back to God! I had to learn that the hard way. God prohibited me from having a social media presence in my beginning stages because he wanted to teach me how to walk in humility. A big head (pride) will make you lose your head (authority). In 1 Kings 18, Elijah is seen defeating false prophets in a showdown on a mountain. In the very next chapter, 1 Kings 19, we then see Elijah wanting to end his prophetic journey in a quiet secluded place. This speaks of his humility. His notoriety could have made him aspire toward trying to take the throne, yet he valued his prophetic mandate over earthly positions.

Elijah did not straddle the fence. He was a man of faith in Yahweh and Yahweh alone. Oftentimes, this is an issue with mainstream prophetic vessels, who are often hot one day and cold the next. But in order to make ready a people prepared for the Lord (Luke 1:17), there must be no compromise. The decision must be made to stand up for righteousness and holiness.

Additionally, Elijah was a man who was willing to step aside when required. He was an individual who considered the future. He was not selfish but was willing to release a double measure onto his spiritual son, Elisha. Prophetic individuals are not now-focused, they must be future-focused. His mindset was to continue a legacy in the earth. The same held true with John the Baptist. He was willing to announce a greater move of the Spirit. Prophetic people who cannot point directly to Jesus have not completed basic training and AIT. When God sends you forth, you are sent as a representative of the Kingdom.

Malachi 4:6 (ESV)

"Behold, I will send you Elijah the prophet before the great and awesome day of the Lord comes. And he will

*turn the hearts of fathers to their children and the hearts
of children to their fathers, lest I come and strike the land
with a decree of utter destruction."*

THE SPIRIT of Elijah comes to bring reconciliation on the earth—both from a natural lens and a spiritual lens. God sends prophets to establish reconnection at the familial level. True transformation will begin in homes. That is why it is gravely important for prophetic individuals to understand that we are the hope at every level of interaction. Christ is not coming to tear apart and separate families; he comes to restore them and bring things into alignment. When God sends prophets, he sends them forth with the mandate to restore and keep families from separating. It is a bad model for churches to connect with the world while losing their individual families. Balance in the prophetic will recalibrate these issues as they come with a word of alignment.

Prophetic Collaborators & Prophetic Oversight

When prophets are sent by God, they have a mandate to collaborate. Too often, individuals embrace loneliness and enjoy working in seclusion. This is anti-apostolic and will ultimately cause things to be built lopsided in the earth. Collaboration releases accountability, apostolic might, and networks that are drenched in the mind of Christ. God sends prophets where He desires for His voice to reign. Sent ones are apostolic in nature, so even prophetic individuals are required to grow and go apostolically. Review the following scripture and see the prophetic and apostolic suggestive: *"But the Lord said to me, 'Do not say, 'I am only a youth;' for to all to whom I send you, you shall go, and whatever I command you, you shall speak. Do not be afraid of them, for I am with you to deliver you,' declares the Lord. Then the Lord put out his hand and touched my mouth. And the Lord said to me, 'Behold, I have put my words in your mouth. See, I have set you this day over nations and over kingdoms, to pluck up and to break down, to destroy and to overthrow, to build and to plant'"* (Jeremiah 1:7-10, ESV).

We see here that God gave Jeremiah the charge to speak His word. There will be prophets who will sit under and collaborate with pastors or executives and release the Word of the Lord. When I was an administrator of a school, I sat under the authority of another administrator; however, I was given the opportunity to oversee the human resources arena of my school. On several occasions, the head principal would ask me for prophetic advice concerning which interviewees I felt "good vibes" from. This was a prophetic pull in the marketplace and business arena. From the general pool of candidates, they knew I had a good radar for selecting the most suitable teaching candidates. Now, I was never called "prophet" at school, but the gift was heavily pulled on when major decisions had to be made. I had to collaborate with others to achieve our common goals. Likewise, your prophetic gift is only respected and utilized in areas where there is usage. No one likes after-the-fact prophets, so you must build strong connections in order to release words ahead of time and build your prophetic resume to establish prophetic tenure.

Although it is important for prophets to be connected to other prophets, it is vital that there be some ministerial diversity. I love prophets, but there will be nothing accomplished in the earth if prophets just came together and spoke the word of God. There are times where prophets should be in communities alone for prophetic development (AIT); however, when God sends prophets, it is for diversity's sake. There is always an agenda of heaven when He sends these officers out in the world.

Prophets often love to pluck up, break down, destroy, and overthrow, yet the latter clause of Jeremiah 1:10 is actually the most important part: it says to build and plant. All too frequently, prophetic people tear down without continuing on to build back up. Think about it: demolition is easy but building and establishing take time and effort. There is an apostolic flavor in the prophetic as there are prophets whose main functions are to build and oversee. There must be an administrative pull on the prophetic. The best people to oversee and teach prophets are other prophets. You are sent by God when you have the skillset and the knowledge to impart and teach what you know. Most of the prophetic types that we see in the Bible had the responsibility to train. Even in their sent areas, they made sure that their prophetic mandate did not die with them. In Elisha's death, he felt the need to tag an individual with resurrection power. True apostolic and prophetic sent ones do not die without marking the next generation to carry on. That is how we ensure that prophetic lineages and ultimately the name of Christ continues on through all generations.

BEING SENT by God is an honor and a privilege. The attributes above equip the prophetic types when God sends them into the combat zone. Just as military bases are located in certain places to establish a physical presence and influence even in times of peace, so too does God place his prophets in places before warfare manifests. Likewise, God will also send them during times of war. There is no better officer and warrior to send than those who have been through basic and AIT. Realize that there have been several people who have been drafted, yet they are not easily trusted by society or by the church due to their novice-like behavior and skill. As you go forth with longevity in mind, it is important that you remember to work together, suit up with integrity, participate in regular maintenance checks, be willing to sacrifice sleep, and double up in prayer when necessary. The examples below are prophetic individuals who were sent on a prophetic assignment by God.

Moses

Exodus 3:10 (ESV)

"Come, I will send you to Pharaoh that you may bring my people, the children of Israel, out of Egypt."

Moses was a prophetic deliverer. God sent him as an official to go and extract his special people out from bondage. His assignment was both regional and international. Moses had to deliver his people from one place to another. Not only did he enter a war zone, but God showed him that his prophetic might was in the voice of the Lord. God sent Moses because his heart was broken as a result of injustice that was occurring to his people. Prophets must not forget civilians because they too are God's sheep. A prophet that has no heart for the people will rarely produce miracles and can strain the hand of God in the places where they have been assigned.

God showed Moses that not only was he a prophet, but he also needed to function pastorally and apostolically in order for the people to be ushered into their promise. Of course, there were complaints and grumbling among the people, however, Moses stayed with his assignment. Likewise, you are charged to carry out God's orders. It may not be easy and those who are called to labor with you may come against you. Yet, your assignment has divine protection attached to it. When you give God a yes, heaven stands in agreement to make sure you accomplish His will in the earth. Consider again the armed forces. When they are deployed and are distressed, they have backup from the one who sent them.

Deborah

Judges 4:4-5 (ESV)

"Now Deborah, a prophetess, the wife of Lappidoth, was judging Israel at that time. She used to sit under the palm of Deborah between Ramah and Bethel in the hill country of Ephraim, and the people of Israel came up to her for judgment."

Deborah was a prophet and a judge that was given

jurisdiction to judge Israel. Her prophetic reach was regional and international. People came to her for judgement as her level of influence was impeccable. She also had the power and strength to inspire others. Not only was her charge prophetic but it was also apostolic and pastoral. She was willing to walk with Barak and be his prophetic guide through warfare. She called for Barak and ignited troops to fight. Additionally, she was able to see in him what he was not able to see in himself. Her prophetic wisdom and experience with God encouraged and was a prophetic guide for Barak. God will send you with the wisdom and strength to deal with people and to usher them into personal, business, and ministerial victory.

John the Baptist

> Matthew 3:1; 5-6 (ESV)
>
> *"In those days John the Baptist came preaching in the wilderness of Judea. Then Jerusalem and all Judea and all the region about the Jordan were going out to him, and they were baptized by him in the river Jordan, confessing their sins."*

John the Baptist was sent into the wilderness. The wilderness is the perfect place for prophets. Not only does God equip those he sends, but he spiritually and physically prepares them where he has placed them. The wilderness often brings out wild devils. John was placed into a combat zone containing religious individuals where there had been a lot of religious contention, yet he stood his ground. When God sends prophets, they are sent to stand even in the midst of adversity. We do not retreat. We are called with the mandate to stand firm on the promises of God. John knew his region and his mandate.

John had a regional mandate but prepared the way for someone who had an international mandate. Additionally, John shows us that when God sends us into regions on assignment, we must be sensitive. Assignments do not last forever and there will be shifts that the prophet must be sensitive to, but always understand that there is safety in your assignment. There will be times where your prophetic voice will be elevated and there will be times that God will raise up others and amplify their voices. Jesus was able to echo that John the Baptist was the greatest prophet born of a woman because he was able to announce with humility that Jesus is coming and that he is greater. John was willing to decrease to see God increase. When you are sent, please know that God must be on center stage and that you are just the vehicle, not the driver!

Conclusion

Prophets are not called to be stuck in basic training and AIT forever. Your assignment and the earth depend on your willingness to measure up, reach the standard of the prophetic, and go forth to change the world. As you enter into your sent realm, you are the change that heaven will bring forth. It will come through your eyes, your ears, and your hands. The 5-fold gifts are people! God gave gifts—in the form of men—to men. When you realize that you are a gift to the world, you will act better and display the character of Christ. It is just like God to make us like him, a gift to humanity. Poor character and a lack of training distorts the beautifully wrapped gift into a damaged and torn box. Glory was wrapped up in Jesus (John 1:14); likewise, the prophetic and glory is wrapped up inside of you for you to make a kingdom impact.

The prophetic went through a major shift between the New and Old Testaments. The next chapter will prepare you so that you function as a New Testament prophetic type instead of the old model.

7

SAME WORLD, DIFFERENT METHODS

There is a clear difference between the prophets who came before John the Baptist and those who came after. Oddly enough, most of the modern church is stuck in an Old Testament prophetic wineskin. This old wine is a deterrent to the move of God and ultimately acts as a dividing agent, instead of a mechanism for unity in most churches and networks. I remember sitting at my father's church about 17 years ago and this very accurate prophetic voice stood up and gave a prophecy. This was the word of the Lord that he gave: "you are filthy, you are stinking to the nostrils of God. How dare you." The word was so sharp, you could cut the atmosphere in the church with a butter knife. Needless to say, the word offended more than it healed. Although the word was accurate and on point, it was laced with an Old Testament mode of delivery. Moving from this realm is not as hard as you think. By the end of this chapter, you will see that the keys to flowing in the new prophetic ministry will rest in the understanding of the Holy Spirit, the cross, unification, mercy and atonement, and proper delivery systems.

John the Baptist was different from the New Testament prophets. The greatest Old Testament prophet is less than the New Testament believer. In Matthew 11:11 (ESV) Jesus says, *"Truly, I say to you, among those born of women there has arisen no one greater than John the Baptist. Yet the one who is least in the kingdom of heaven is greater than he."* There is an evident change in humanity when Jesus came on the scene. Consider briefly the understanding of the Holy Spirit. Prophets of old are different in administration and function, and they had limits and barriers because they were people who received empowerment "on" them instead of "in" them. The fact that we harness both the intrinsic and extrinsic power of the Holy Spirit gives us an advantage in the Kingdom. There are many examples of believers having both the Holy Spirit in them and his presence on or over them.

Even Jesus, fully God and fully man, quoted the prophet Isaiah in Luke 4:18-19 (ESV) when he said, *"The Spirit of the Lord is upon me, because he has anointed me to proclaim good news to the poor. He has sent me to proclaim liberty to the captives and recovering of sight to the blind, to set at liberty those who are oppressed, to proclaim the year of the Lord's favor."* After Jesus' death on the cross, something major happen. What was once on believers and prophets now came to reside inside of them. Having the Holy Spirit in us means that we should display the nature and the characteristics of Christ. This also proves that the prophetic became a byproduct of the death of Christ. Hearing is not exclusive to prophets or something that only prophets can hold as a trophy. Hearing became the language of relationship and the responsibility of all Christians.

In the Old Testament, the people relied on the prophets of God alone to hear and give direction to Israel. Although New Testament prophets can direct the church, they are not the only ones who can discern, see, and hear what God is saying. The throne room of heaven is open to all sons. One of the dangers of trying to recreate Old Testament prophetic ministry in modern times is the exclusivity that is breeds. When the veil was ripped, access became available for all. Prophets who have an old flavor often give off the impression that they are the only ones who God talks to. Furthermore, their focus is judgement and damnation. There is such a hyper focus on judgement and the law that people feel they can never measure up to the standard. I remember when I was growing up that was the only expectation of prophets when they came into churches: to speak about sin. Although sin is real and should be preached, there is a better method to reduce sin than preaching and nailing people to the law and the judgement of God.

New Testament prophetics carries a message of hope. It is laced with the reconciliatory power of God. When prophets with a New Testament stance speak the mind of God, it will leave one with the understanding that God is reaching out to them, not for a death sentence but to change their life. The 5-fold ministry gifts are for the equipping of the saints and for the work of the ministry (Ephesians 4:11). This is important to understand because the focus of New Testament prophetics does not position an individual in the way, but instead moves them out of the way. Many prophetic ministers stand in the way of God forming relationships with individuals by always being the voice that people turn to whenever they need to hear what God is saying. New Testament prophetics has a keen interest in individuals developing their own ability to hear the voice of God. True modern prophetic ministry is all about Jesus!

Prophetic ministry took a 180 degree turn when Jesus came around. While the Old Testament was an invitation of the coming King to overthrow and other civilizations, the New Testament prophetic ministry has unification and salvation at the forefront of its mandate. I have seen countless prophetic vessels split churches, break up marriages, and sow seeds of discord and suspicion. Prophetic ministry is a unifying agent for the local church. If prophets began to understand this mandate then every pastor would want a prophet to serve on their leadership, head certain auxiliaries, and preach. Yet, in most charismatic circles, prophets parade around with a peacock spirit, where they want grand entrances to the best seats, take up large honorariums, and prophesy for lucrative gain.

It is amazing how Jesus said that John the Baptist was the greatest prophet born of a woman. He announced Jesus and gave the people a baptism of repentance. This was the transition of something spectacular in the earth. John's head had to be severed so that the head of the church could emerge. The role of the prophet had to shift in order for people to see Jesus. If prophets continued to minister from a place of vengeance, law, and judgement, we would still need a sacrifice. Jesus' blood and entrance in the earth shifted everything. Jesus walking on the earth meant that people did not need a mediator; they could hear the voice of God for themselves. I honestly believe that is why the Old Testament is filled with stories of prophets, while the New Testament is filled with sons who cry out to Abba, Father. The most important role in everything is a son. The New Testament prophetic shows the body of Christ how to receive an inheritance and walk in sonship. Doing so will upgrade people from hyper sin consciousness to son consciousness, something that will ultimately defeat the presence and the power of sin.

Abel is the first Old Testament example that we have while Jesus is the first New Testament example. Hebrews 12:24 (ESV) states, *"and to Jesus, the mediator of a new covenant, and to the sprinkled blood that speaks a better word than the blood of Abel."* Both of these men acted as prophetic intercessors standing in between God and humanity. One's response to blood was totally different than the other's. There must be a change in perspective as it relates to hurt, trauma, isolation, and rejection. Recently, I was traveling with a prophet friend named Jacob who had just caught wind that someone was talking badly about him. The individual that was trash talking was a born-again believer. His salvation does not mean that it was acceptable, but it just added more fuel to the fire for Jacob. In response, Jacob called on the vengeance and judgement of God to literally come and take the person out. The person did say some awful things; however, Jacob's response was from an Old Testament model. Clearly, the thing that hangs in the balance between the New Testament and Old Testament prophet is the nature and character of Christ. A person who is immature in their walk with Christ will easily revert back to Old Testament prophetic practices.

Interestingly enough, the comparison of blood mentioned in the previous scripture is between two prophets and their response to trauma. One prophet cried out in for vengeance and justice while the other cried out for mercy and grace. Thus, all modern-day prophets should lace their function with deep intercession and mercy for humanity. Some individuals can be so dogmatic and judgmental that their lens is only gloom and doom, causing them to prophesy at the cross and not from the cross. Your biblical stance and understanding of the intent of the Father will be the model for all of your prophetic words. Prophets who do not understand that Jesus was the atonement for our sins will make their constituents the atonement. Prophets who understand Jesus as the perfect sacrifice will use the prophetic as an olive branch into the Kingdom and not a master's whip for slaves.

There should be a generation of prophetic people who can look at those who are lost or backslidden and prophesy hope and the light of Christ with such an evangelistic flavor that individuals are convicted of change and not fussed out of change. I have heard so many prophets who have a fear-based method. This method has been long outdated and has led people to shun God instead of running right into His arms. Fear and reverence are two different things. We should reverence God, but fear should be removed because fear cancels out faith. And faith is directly connected to the ears and the eyes of the spirit. Faith comes by hearing and hearing by the word of God (Romans

10:17). When there is fear, words are received incorrectly, attitude is given, and people hide instead of standing naked and unashamed. Notice that the criteria to evaluate new testament prophetics is not whether or not a word comes to pass; instead, it is whether the word edifies, exhorts, and comforts.

Also, Old Testament prophetics do not include the realm of judging prophetic words. Whether a prophet was off or not was based on whether a prophet's word came into fruition. If the word did not come to pass, it was a sign that the prophet was off. Deuteronomy 18:20-22 (ESV) says, *"But the prophet who presumes to speak a word in my name that I have not commanded him to speak, or who speaks in the name of other gods, that same prophet shall die.' And if you say in your heart, 'How may we know the word that the Lord has not spoken?'— when a prophet speaks in the name of the Lord, if the word does not come to pass or come true, that is a word that the Lord has not spoken; the prophet has spoken it presumptuously. You need not be afraid of him."* Notice here that death was required of prophets who attempted to speak for God when he had not commanded them to speak. This is for the blatant intent to speak without hearing, not for those who heard and simply got it wrong. It is impossible to judge a prophetic word right on the spot because an individual is standing in the present releasing a word for the future. So, the New Testament judging of prophetic words extends beyond something coming to pass. The prophetic rubric for New Testament prophetics involves relationship, nature, fruit, and unity. Consequently, the words of a prophet are vetted and judged in the sight of other prophetic vessels to ensure that the nature of a Christly delivery system is at work.

Conclusion

There are clear distinctions between Old and New Testament prophetics. Jesus gives us a perfect example after the disregard and disrespect he receives from various people in Luke 9:51-56. The disciples asked if they should call down fire (judgement). Jesus rebuked them, giving them a different prophetic stance. This is a learning moment for every callous prophet. Even though you can, it does not mean you should. There is jurisdiction that God has given us as prophetic vessels, and we must be great stewards over this. Always remember that Christ comes to seek and save the lost, even those who are in the house and still lost. Embrace this New Testament anointing. It is less stressful, yields better results, and will please the Father because reconciliation and unity have always been his goal, even before the beginning of the earth.

GIFT, SPIRIT, & OFFICE

This is the age in which God is restoring the apostolic and the prophetic gifts in the body of Christ. Because of this, there have been heightened levels of misidentification of these offices. There are individuals who simply step into these offices because they can "prophesy." There are also leaders who desire to become more prophetic and ignorantly align themselves with prophetic individuals, reading prophetic material, and ultimately camouflaging themselves because this office seems glamorous. Some do this knowingly while others do so under an illusion, morphing their identities in order to become super spiritual instead of identifying their real purpose and fulfilling their own mandates in the earth. It is critical that we enhance ordination and commissioning criteria so that the sanctity and output of these offices regain their accreditation, both naturally and spiritually.

As a young, saved Christian, I never told anyone I was a prophet. At a very young age I received a prophecy detailing my calling and mandate. Be mindful, my future was affirmed in the early 1990s. This was a time when the prophetic was far from the mainstream and not something that was desirable due to the degree of the scrutiny and warfare that came along with it. There is always going to be demonic warfare as well as friendly fire from other brothers and sisters in Christ who lack understanding regarding prophets and the prophetic ministry. Fortunately, as a child, my parents understood and guided my maturation as a child of God. Like Mary pulling Jesus back as a teen in the temple, but later thrusting him forth into ministry at a wedding, it takes discerning individuals around you to help usher you into your full mandate (Luke 2:51; John 2:1-5). My parents understood the timeframe between calling and commissioning. This in between time is called process. Contrary to popular belief, prophets are born first and then made. A prophetic individual that has been born to prophesy but not fashioned by the hand of God can easily slip into the hands of the devil, trading their mantle for a moment of fame. Prophets are fashioned by the hand of God through God's training system (Desert Storm). Their gifts must be awakened, and full maturation must occur before they are full-bodied office prophets. When an individual becomes the office, there is a certain level of acumen that is expected. Be assured that prophets do not own prophecy, nor is prophecy reserved for prophets exclusively.

Gift of Prophecy

Before we discuss the gift of prophecy, we must understand what prophecy is. In its purest form, prophecy is words inspired by a deity. As it relates to Christians, true prophets or prophetic individuals speak on behalf of God. Some of the things that we have deemed as prophecy are merely components of prophecy. The church correlates the calling out of names, numbers, and dates to prophecy. Now, those things can be used in the scope and realm of prophecy, but they alone are not sufficient enough to say that they are the word of the Lord. The apostle Paul gave us a great frame for prophecy; according to 1 Corinthians 14:3 (ESV), *"but he who prophesies speaks to people for their upbuilding and encouragement and consolation."* This is powerful to understand because when one stands to declare the word of God, it should be a building tool so that the church can be built up. Although prophets are people of holiness and righteous living, even after the calling out of sin, there must be a building up. Leaving judgement dangling from a prophetic word that tore people down is a faulty prophetic mindset.

Jeremiah 1:9-10 (ESV)

"*Then the Lord put out his hand and touched my mouth. And the Lord said to me, 'Behold, I have put my words in your mouth. See, I have set you this day over nations and over kingdoms, to pluck up and break down, to destroy and to overthrow, to build and to plant.'*"

EVEN FROM AN OLD TESTAMENT LENS, the prophet was used to build and to plant. As vessels, we must ensure that things are made better and not worse because of our prophetic proclamations. Ultimately, it is wise to be an instrument to strengthen a local church. I have seen countless prophets who have been asked to preach at churches. They ignorantly have used this as an opportunity to attack the people. When a person solicits you to minister, it should always be to strengthen that local house. Words are powerful; we must use them to nourish people. Doing so will cause people to start to honor prophecy and local pastors will begin to welcome prophets again. Oddly enough, immature prophets have caused a setback for the prophetic movement, dating back to the 1990s.

The gift of prophecy is a gift given by the Holy Spirit. This gift enables an individual to give utterance.

The gift of prophecy requires a mouth, and it requires faith. It is a speaking gift and requires language. This is a gift of the Holy Spirit, so, anyone with the Holy Spirit can access it; however, generally, prophets steward this gift better. While others must have an unction to release what God is saying, generally those with a strong prophetic grace or calling can find this quite easy. Interestingly enough, Paul tells the church to desire this gift (1 Corinthians 14:1). God will not tell you to desire something that could not be fulfilled. The apostle Paul's admonishment to desire prophecy will inevitably set the church up to be empowered and perfected. God promised to give us the desires of our heart (Psalms 37:4). The more I seek God, the more desires he puts in me. One of these is for prophecy. Prophecy is a building tool for the church and for believers. Consider this: if there is so much building that is needed in the body of Christ, prophecy is the tool that can accomplish it.

Many people flow seamlessly through this gift. Accessing prophecy does not mean that an individual is a prophet. The New Testament was comprised of individuals who prophesied. There are countless examples of people receiving the Holy Spirit and prophecies. Thus, being full of the Holy Spirit will enable individuals to be inspired to speak. An individual that possesses and operates in this gift must be careful because it attracts a lot of attention from bystanders. The church and the world are enamored by individuals who can see and declare the future. Consider you own city and how many tarot card and palm readers it has. Humans love to be in the "know." Thus, this gift is often bought, used for selfish gain, pimped, borrowed, and misused, causing much unnecessary division among the saints.

Spirit of Prophecy

> Revelations 19:9-10 (ESV)
>
> "And the angel said to me, 'Write this: Blessed are those who are invited to the marriage supper of the Lamb.' And he said to me, 'These are the true words of God.' Then I fell down at his feet to worship him, but he said to me, 'You must not do that! I am a fellow servant with you and your brothers who hold the testimony of Jesus. Worship God.' For the testimony of Jesus is the Spirit of Prophecy."

This scripture speaks to how individuals should handle prophecy and the operation of prophecy. The apostle John wrote about his encounter with an angel. This angel came and delivered a word from God. John fell down and began to worship the messenger. This is a dangerous response to encounters with individuals who speak on behalf of God. Honestly, I believe this is why the prophetic ministry has taken a downward spiral: people began to worship the messenger. God's word is true that he will not have any other god before him. As prophetic ministers, our duty is to connect people to Christ and Christ alone. Pointing people to ourselves is a fallacy that will cause major damage. Not only is it detrimental for the person worshipping the prophet, but it is equally as treacherous for the prophet. Every idol in the Bible came down; Dagon is a good example. He was left on the ground without a head and limbs (1 Samuel 5:2-5). Likewise, God will remove false idols and anything else that stands in the way.

All prophecy should be connected to Jesus. The testimony of Jesus is the vehicle that prophecy should flow from. First, a prophetic word will point to Jesus. It will connect to his divine purpose for individuals. Secondly, it gives us the power of prophecy. Jesus' testimony is triumphant in nature. There was nothing that stood in his way. Additionally, demonic oppositions were obsolete. This lets us know that prophecy has resurrection power. No matter what we discern or see, prophecy has a plot twist for anything negative that can be detected. When you stand as an oracle of God to declare his word, there is always a triumphant ending for His Bride. There is redemptive power in the testimony of Jesus, giving the bold proclamation that there is nothing too challenging for the believer.

If it is Jesus' testimony, then all prophecy will be initiated by the Holy Spirit and will be about Him. It takes the Holy Spirit to prophesy. The Holy Spirit is the spirit of Christ. John 14:19-20 (ESV) states, *"Yet a little hole and the world will see me no more, but you will see me. Because I live, you also will live. In that day you will know that I am in my Father, and you in me, and I in you."* The Holy Spirit gives individuals the gift of prophecy. Additionally, it is the Holy Spirit that speaks through individuals and allows them to utter. The spirit of prophecy can fill a room. This is an occurrence in which the atmosphere is pregnant with the words of God. Typically, anyone sensitive or connected will begin to prophesy. Consider Saul who encountered a prophetic company. The spirit of prophecy was upon him and he prophesied and was considered among the prophets. This is very likely to occur in a prophetic church. Individuals will easily flow because the spirit of prophecy will be on them. There is a distinct difference from prophesying from an atmospheric charge and from an inward prophetic charge. An atmospheric charge is contingent upon the Holy Spirit coming in a room with other prophetic vessels, while an inward prophetic charge can come from the inside at any moment. People that are filled with the Holy Spirit can change and charge the atmosphere. God desires for you to be a prophetic game changer!

Office

Oftentimes we refer to prophets as "walking in the office." In all actuality, however, this terminology does not describe the fullness of this five-fold gift. The individual does not walk in anything; they are the office. A five-fold gift is an actual person. An officer is someone with authority, jurisdiction, and rank, who represents a kingdom. All five-fold ministers are officers for the Kingdom of God. They transact business and ensure that the body of Christ complies with the word. According to Ephesians 4:11-24, these officers are called to grow the Church and help it mature. It takes established individuals to complete this duty. The immature cannot bring others into maturity.

All five-fold ministers are called by God, but self-appointed prophets are more common than you would assume. In a lot of apostolic structures, individuals will make people prophets in order to look as if they are complete. I have also witnessed people being confirmed as prophets because they were the most prophetic individual in a church. This is gravely hideous to the sanctity of this mandate. No one can make a person a prophet. It is the Lord who calls, and He does so from an eternal posture. Although some individuals are called prophets or born prophets, there is a proper time for the fullness of that word to come into fruition. Prophets are people who love righteousness. They sit in the counsel of God. They are people of justice and are people of the word. Logos and rhema are equally important to prophets. Prophets are individuals who release the word of God, however, there are several examples that reveal this is a lower function to the prophetic call. For example, Abel and John the Baptist both have no recorded examples of prophecy, yet John the Baptist was recorded as the greatest prophet born of a woman.

Prophecy became a responsibility for the believer and the prophet's office became an administrative and executive function for the church. One of the main objectives of prophets is to train people how to hear the voice of God. Prophets are not the sole authority in churches; however, they collaborate and submit their gift to the leadership of the church. Oftentimes prophets are upset or walk in offense because what they see is not necessarily followed through with. It is imperative that prophets understand that apostles and pastors can see as well. It takes all things for the church to move forward. Lastly, it is vital for prophets to receive deliverance. A prophetic word must bypass two levels before it comes out: soul and the flesh. The spirit is pure, yet a damaged soul can alter the prophetic word causing it to be off or lose authenticity. Prophets should be mature instructors for upcoming prophetic vessels. This will raise the prophetic standard in the Kingdom.

Conclusion

It is vital that people walk in their own lanes. Head-on collisions occur when people enter into the wrong lane. People who erroneously access the office of the Prophet create unnecessary damage for churches and organizations. The objective is to be prophetic. We all can be that by the Holy Spirit. So, the gift and the spirit of prophecy is something that everyone walk in! BOOM! Now, there is a measure given to everyone. So, if you only have two words, be faithful over those two. If you have two paragraphs, deliver them well. Do it all with the same intensity, knowing that God is the one that you will have to give account to. Everyone who prophesies is not a prophet. Accuracy is not an indication of a prophet. Allow God to process and take you through various stages of prophetic development. The office of the prophet is not for everyone. Let me say that again: it is not for everyone. It is for those who God has called before the foundation of the world. This is serious business and should be handled with care, poise, and dignity.

NOTES

2. The Call to Intercession

1. "H8104 - šāmar - Strong's Hebrew Lexicon (KJV)." Blue Letter Bible. Accessed 19 Feb, 2021. https://www.blueletterbible.org//lang/lexicon/lexicon.cfm?Strongs=H8104&t=KJV

ABOUT THE AUTHOR

Apostle Charlie Howell III was born and raised in eastern North Carolina. He holds degrees in Biblical Studies and History Education, and a Master's Degree in School Administration. He served in public schools as an assistant principal for four years and as a teacher for four years. He desires to see the people of God empowered and the Body of Christ come into the perfect being, as described by Apostle Paul in Ephesians 4:11-13.

Apostle Charlie established Kingdom Now Embassy (KNE) in 2015. KNE is an organization that empowers people in the realm of education and personal responsibility. KNE has a local church expression called Eastern North Carolina (ENC) Hub. Apostle Charlie is also the founder of a K-12 private Christian school called Embassy Innovation Academy. The school's objective is to educate children to think outside the box with a solid biblical foundation. As the founder of Howell Global, LLC, Apostle Charlie has a goal to release Kingdom apparel, education, and mentorship. Apostle is the creator of the Shamar Institute, which has a focus on raising up modern day apostles and prophets. Apostle Charlie is married to Shanda Howell, and together they have four children: Josiah (our angel), Charlee, Charlie IV, and Charleigh.

Apostle seeks to cross denominations, cultures, and various ethnic groups to spread the Gospel of Jesus Christ and thrust people into their destinies. He is an advocate for prayer, prophecy, holiness, and righteous living. He strives to lead by example and display the love of God in his everyday life.

Made in the USA
Columbia, SC
27 June 2021

40708771R00095